TOUGH
TIMES
HANDBOOK

TOUGH TIMES
HANDBOOK

A BLUEPRINT FOR BUSINESS SURVIVAL

NICHOLAS BATE

The right of Nicholas Bate to be identified as the author of this book has been asserted in accordance with the Copyright, Designs and Patents Act 1988.

Woodslane Press
An imprint of Business & Professional Publishing Pty Ltd
Unit 7/5 Vuko Place
Warriewood NSW 2102
Australia
Email: info@woodslane.com.au
Website: www.woodslane.com.au

First published in 2008 by
The Infinite Ideas Company Limited
This Edition published 2008 by Woodslane Press
Copyright © Infinite Ideas Limited , 2008

The information in this publication is based upon the current state of commercial and industry practice, applicable legislation, general law, and the general circumstances as at the date of publication. No person shall rely on any of the contents of this publication and the publisher and the author expressly exclude all liability for direct and indirect loss suffered by any person resulting in any way from the use of or reliance on this publication or any part of it. Any opinions and advice are offered solely in pursuance of the author's and publisher's intention to provide information, and have not been specifically sought.

National Library of Australia Cataloguing-in-Publication entry

Bate, Nicholas
Tough Times Handbook: a blueprint for business survival /Nicholas Bate

ISBN: 9781921203626 (pbk.)

Includes index.

Success in business.
Business planning.

650.1

Designed and typeset by Baseline Arts Ltd, Oxford
Printed and bound in China through Colorcraft Ltd, Hong Kong

Contents

● ●

Introduction

A recession is strictly defined as two or more quarters of declining growth. As I write world markets appear to be heading that way rapidly, with the USA close to confirming that status and recent on the Asia stock markets compounding the effects of inflation already present in that area. The UK and Europe are suffering badly with generally poor High Street trading and a stalled housing market.

The predictions are that tough times are ahead, which is why you must act now.

You know the frog in the boiling water story don't you? Put a frog in boiling water and it jumps out: it reacts, it takes action, the frog does something. Of course, it would! What about the manager of a small OD consultancy? Wakes up on a Monday morning, picks up his *Financial Review* and it is framed in black. The lead story is about the biggest stock market fall since records began, how house prices have dropped by 30% in two weeks. He gets into the office and his in-box is full of cancelled orders. Yes – I know. It's a 'no-brainer'. He'd take non-stop 100% action wouldn't he?

Now the manager of a small Italian restaurant hears that Myer (after several excellent years) has had a dreadful Christmas. Oh, and by the way – he hears – the USA is (many analysts consider) in full recession. Oh and by the way – he notices – the housing market has stalled. Oh and by the way (one of his few September customers mentions) new car sales are considerably down. Oh and by the way

– he reflects – foot-fall in his restaurant this August has been unusually low. Oh well. Maybe it'll work itself out. A cappuccino, please.

No, no, no – I don't think so. And I'm certain you are not thinking like that. *You* are going to take action. The bigger your business, the longer it's going to take to turn it around, and the earlier you need to start. If you are a one-man band you've got to keep bringing in revenue while making these changes.

ACT NOW

Act to make your business as robust as possible. In times of growth, you can lose a bit of margin here and there, you can carry one or two under-performers. Debtor days at 60? Well, it's not ideal but the bank's supporting us. How many contractors are there working on that project? Nobody's quite sure! But there are plenty of sales – all heavily discounted of course. All of the above are fine when the economy is growing but when it stalls bad business practices become exposed.

And there's the rub: a recession exposes our poor working practices. This blueprint for survival, this plan for success will take you through exactly the points you need to follow to get back on track in a way that you know makes sense for now and the future.

In the chapters that follow, we'll address **money issues** and make sure you get the cash you need more quickly. We'll ensure you maximise your margin and profit and stop silly discounting. We'll look at how to find new sources of profitable business and stop the bad payers. In particular we'll show how to avoid a slippery slope of discounting and deals, which is the panic reaction of many at such a time, but all it will do is send you to the wall. It requires good planning and nerve; we'll help you with both.

We'll take you step by step through the **tough decisions** that need to be made about product and customers who are losing you money and under-performers in the team, and suppliers, who are, quite frankly, distracting you from what you do best. Delay on these tough decisions and you will rapidly become exposed. Act quickly and you could find that the recession is genuinely a time of opportunity for you.

We'll discuss **the facts** you need to make great decisions. Facts regarding who and what makes the money in your consultancy or at your factory. We'll give you the knowledge to help you see which sales people are worth three of the others. And we'll show you how to spot a great deal. Too many businesses, too much of the time, make decisions based on guesswork – not you: knowledge is power.

When we focus in on **people**, we'll remind you what really motivates them: because it's not simply money. We'll give you ideas that will enable you to get a lot more out of (probably) a lot fewer people – and have them enjoying themselves, too.

Absolutely critically we'll get right back to real **selling** –handling price concerns, proper negotiation. We'll focus on real targets of profitability not just revenue, and developing accounts not just taking orders. We'll show you the benefits of a proper pipeline and forecasting system, which lead to predictability of business.

If you thought **marketing** was a luxury in a recession, we'll show you how it truly comes into its own. You thought the 4Ps were just for academics? Absolutely not. We'll review how to position and price for the growth you want. Pricing elasticity is mere jargon – we'll show you how to price properly.

We've all heard that 'the devil is in the detail' but the phrase you need to live by now is 'be **brilliant at the basics**'. Get a lot of basics right: phone answering, cheque chasing, friendly reception, accurate shipping and you have an excellent business. And there aren't enough of those around, which is good news for you.

There's some tough **communicating** to do all round. We'll summarise how to do it: the bad news, the grim news and the good news.

When it comes to finding **opportunities** you are already ahead of the game. Some of your competitors have hardly woken up to what's really happening out there and are going to really struggle: that's good news for you. We'll show you how to grab every opportunity.

Time management was a challenge before the downturn. And now? Let's get clear on the critical difference between working *in* your business and *on* your business. Study this blueprint and that's great *on* time. The start of a lot you're going to be doing.

You'll need some **fun** because without it you'll all burn out, but fun need not be expensive at all.

The way out of this recession is to **innovate**. Innovation is creativity plus action. Perhaps you have not thought of yourself as creative before but we'll show you that you are and how to take action and mesh the two complementary skills for a powerful new organisation.

With fewer people you need great working **processes and systems**. The more you can automate the better so we'll help you work out what systems you need to devise and how to improve the one you have: quickly and effectively.

What about you – yes, **the management?** How can you help? Easy: great leadership, cool management and brilliant coaching. These are the soft skills which turn out, in times like this, to have real hard benefits. We'll give you guidance.

The panic option is often to strip back your systems to their bare minimum to reduce costs but what you really need to do is **invest.** Spend wisely of course, but without investment you'll be in no shape when you come out the other side. We'll guide you on which investments you should make.

Stop talking and start acting. This blueprint is 100% action based. No waffle: just guidance. But you can relax. It really will be OK and you will come out of it leaner, meaner and stronger if you start here and now. This book contains the best of current thinking on how to survive – and with care, thrive in – tough times. It is entirely practical: there is absolutely no padding. You know where to find that and you don't want it. There are no pictures, stories or anecdotes. Just 100% turn-this-business-around-now value.

HOW TO USE THIS BOOK

Step 1   Take this book and a highlighter pen to a quiet area for one hour. Highlight all the areas which you need to address. Alongside each topic is a space where you can note your specific customised action. What needs to be done in your business? Who can action it? What are the priorities?

Step 2   Get the management team (that may of course just be you) together. Review your thoughts. Get full buy-in. Assign every action to an individual with a report-back date. Set a date for the next meeting, when those actions will be reviewed.

Step 3 Keep the cycle going. Review and report back at least once a week. If things are very difficult, then do it every day.

Step 4 Come out of tough times a stronger, more streamlined and successful enterprise.

Right – let's make a start.

1. Money!

'City heading for toughest times in a generation, says banking survey. …City firms, especially stockmarket traders, were also gloomy, with many arguing that the next few months could be the toughest in a generation, according to a study of the financial sector.'
Guardian 7 January 2008

● ●

The consensus is that the tough times have arrived, that it will hit all sectors and that it is going to get worse before it gets better. So what's the biggest issue for all of us? Money.

SORTING OUT YOUR FINANCES

Your primary need is to get more money in, more quickly while letting less of t out, more slowly. You need to protect your margin and profit and this means you need to stop silly discounting. Instead find new sources of profitable business and other sources off unding. You need to stop the bad payers and make good money. Here's how.

1. Educate everybody (including yourself, perhaps!) about price

The good news is that it isn't really about price. Just think for a moment about the town or city in which you work. How much is it for a latte to go? Correct: a whole range of prices exists. Are they all fair and just? Yes, because people are willing to pay these prices if they seem to give value for money. So don't panic and slash prices, because you don't necessarily need to change them. What you do need to do is build value.

Consider ideas such as:

- Not discounting at all (e.g. if your business is a restaurant);

- Reducing or even eliminating offers such as 3 for 2 (e.g. if you are a bookseller);

- Reducing the generous deals for volume (e.g. if you run a consultancy).

Perhaps you're thinking, 'but everybody does it and it's expected'. However, that's why everybody's losing money and these tough times will finally bring them down. Get out of that spiral of price-cutting now.

KEY MESSAGE – Stop talking price as there is no correct price. Talk and defend your value. Set your prices confidently. Stop discounting without thought

What **ACTION** do you need to take? Capture it here...

2. Educate everybody (including yourself, perhaps!) about margin

Let's say you sell a product for $100 and the cost is $50. What is your margin? $50 – correct. You now offer 20% discount. So the new price is $80. So what's your new margin? $30. And how much margin did you lose? 40% (note: not 20%)! Frightening isn't it? And so easily done. Make sure those who you allow to negotiate discount have done the calculations and know what they are doing. A deal is only any good if it is making you money. And be very careful about rationalisations such as 'this was a strategic deal', 'this will help market share'. Bullshit: is it making you money?

KEY MESSAGE – Calculate your margins and preserve your profit. Make sure you know who's giving discount and why.

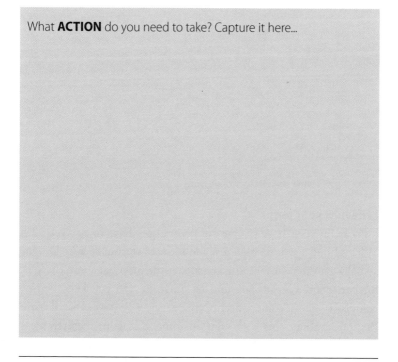

What **ACTION** do you need to take? Capture it here...

3. Do you really need all those deals?

Every deal can become a variation; every variation snags the system. Every snag to the system costs money. Make sure you really want those weird and wonderful deals that are being agreed. Perhaps, on reflection, you don't want the customers who insist on those odd deals. Maybe it would be worth finding customers who will buy sensibly. They are out there. Keep looking.

KEY MESSAGE – Stop doing deals. Search out good customers.

What **ACTION** do you need to take? Capture it here...

4. Review your terms

How many days have people got before they have to pay you? 30? What about if you made it 25? How clear are your terms? Do you actually get the customer to acknowledge them? What about charging for bad debt? Get it clear and be up front. Do you keep getting complaints about some aspect of your service? Postage? Installation? Be honest about this with your customers. It won't frighten away good customers, but it will weed out at an early stage those who are going to be bad news anyway.

KEY MESSAGE – Get your terms clear and make sure the customer agrees to them.

What **ACTION** do you need to take? Capture it here...

5. Chase money at every stage

You know that lack of profit rarely destroys a viable business, but lack of cash certainly can. Ensure the customer knows when they have to pay: get them to acknowledge your terms (see 4 above). Chase them to ensure they have received the invoice and all is OK. Ask when the bill will be paid; assuming they reply that they will pay according to your terms, thank them for that. Chase them the day payment should have been received. Then chase every day until it is paid. Will that lose you a customer? No – because they need you. And if they do go elsewhere that's because they cannot pay you anyway.

KEY MESSAGE – Chase your invoice and confirm it has been received and is OK. Then chase your payment.

What **ACTION** do you need to take? Capture it here...

6. Talk to the bank – early and often

I know you don't like your bank, nor the account person who looks after you, but forget it: you need them. Build the best working relationship you can. Be squeaky clean on keeping them informed over cash flow problems. Have more meetings rather than fewer : ask them how you can reduce bank charges. Keep asking them for better terms. Acknowledge their calls. If you are not getting proper attention ask for someone else to look after your account. Be very wary of trying to change your bank in the middle of a slump; another bank will probably not want your problems. Make it work where you are.

KEY MESSAGE – Build the best relationship you can with your current bank.

What **ACTION** do you need to take? Capture it here...

7. Treat your suppliers with respect

Your suppliers are having problems too. Don't treat them badly or act as if they are stupid. Get in there early and ask if you can lengthen payment terms, say from 30 to 45 days. Do it as early as possible, before others ask. But once you've done that do pay on time. If you have a cash flow problem, ring them up and offer part payment. Work with them, otherwise you might find your business is brought down not by lack of cash but by a missing component for your product.

KEY MESSAGE – Build the best relationship you can with each of your suppliers.

What **ACTION** do you need to take? Capture it here...

8. Manage costs

Make sure you know the cost of *everything*: servicing the fleet of company cars, free bottled water, electricity, stationery – everything. Give someone the task of getting those costs down. There will be cheaper pens for the stationery cupboard, and there will be someone who is willing to do a better deal on your computer maintenance. Just ensure it is like for like and that lower cost does not mean you lose an important component or compromise quality. For a couple of months analyse expenses. Find out where the money goes. Find out who, if anybody, is signing and checking them. Introduce expenses guidelines and ask people to stick to them. Model good behaviours at senior levels; are you really above using public transport?

KEY MESSAGE – Get a handle on every cost and wherever possible, reduce it but stay sensible.

What **ACTION** do you need to take? Capture it here...

9. Stop waste

Heating and lighting. Photocopy paper. Too many sandwiches at lunch-time meetings. Plane tickets bought late at a premium. Hotel expenses. Give clear guidelines. Make it easier not to waste, for example get the photocopier repaired; recommend a site for booking travel tickets.

KEY MESSAGE – Get a handle on every area of waste and remove it.

What **ACTION** do you need to take? Capture it here...

10. Access extra funds

When you need money talk to the bank about every idea possible such as overdraft extensions, business loans and factoring. Also ask friends and family if any of them are willing to invest. Go wider and see if any of your suppliers or customers would be willing to invest. Take care though: if you are feeling vulnerable you may be tempted to be over-generous. One day this nightmare will be over. Will you be happy that you gave away 60% of your business to the in-laws?

> **KEY MESSAGE – Search every avenue for extra funds.** Start with the bank and then widen your search.

What **ACTION** do you need to take? Capture it here...

11. Don't be daft

Stopping the free coffee will save money, but is the annoyance factor more damaging? If you are going to stop coffee for your staff, what pain is the management team enduring? Does the change need to be that dramatic; could the coffee still be subsidised, but not fully?

Before you issue a mandate requiring all staff on business trips to use budget hotels, remember that many of these are in awkward locations and you may simply cause taxi fares to shoot up.

KEY MESSAGE – Be rational.

What **ACTION** do you need to take? Capture it here...

12. Ask for money-saving/making ideas

Ask everyone to come up with ideas: make it easy for them to contribute them both openly and privately. Ask for ideas on how to save money and/or make money. Mention the ones you use and reward those who put the ideas forward. If things get very tough ask them for ideas on reducing salaries and/or bonuses for a 6-month period.

KEY MESSAGE – Ask and encourage great ideas.

What **ACTION** do you need to take? Capture it here...

13. Use students

Those doing business degrees are keen to get real work for their portfolio; they will often work at budget rates and/or part-time in order to gain real-world business experience. Interview and find the smart and enthusiastic ones who do not need much guidance from you. Give them key practical jobs such as proofreading, chasing money, photocopying, answering the phone, researching leads. Keep your key people doing the key stuff.

KEY MESSAGE – Talk to your local college about part-time help from enthusiastic young business people.

What **ACTION** do you need to take? Capture it here...

14. Use the internet

Regularly search the internet for articles and blogs with ideas and tips for survival: after all, one brilliant idea every so often is all you need. Try to identify one idea every week which either helps you make more money, gets it in more quickly, saves money or releases it more slowly. Also use the internet to gain initial ideas on business challenges (for example, what to do about a bad payer) before you start spending serious money with your solicitor.

KEY MESSAGE – Use the internet for zero cost ideas and support.

What **ACTION** do you need to take? Capture it here...

Tough times means that attention to your lifeblood – cash – and an eye on the ultimate goal – profit – cannot be half-hearted. Focus on getting cash in, stopping money wastage and building profitability. That way not only will you survive, you will also thrive.

2. Facts

'Hong Kong – Asian shares closed mixed on Friday after recovering from panic selling triggered by US economic woe as investors pinned their hopes on urgent moves to avoid recession in the world's largest economy.

President George W. Bush was due later on Friday to announce temporary, short-term measures to boost the ailing US economy, a key buyer of Asian goods. The moves were expected to include tax breaks and rebates.'
Straits Times 18 January 2008

● ●

The consensus is that the tough times have arrived, that it will hit all sectors and that it is going to get worse before it gets better. To manage it, to survive it, to ultimately thrive: you have got to have the facts on which you can build your strategies.

FACING FACTS

If you don't already know, find out where the best money comes from in your business. Know which deals are great, and which are bad. Know what is happening in your market now and will happen as the economy declines. Which suppliers give you added extras? Which salespeople are performing? You must have the facts at your fingertips. Here's how.

1. Knowledge is power

You have always known this, but now it is critical. You don't actually know how much margin you made on that deal? Oh! You're not actually sure what this month's travel expenses will be? Mmm. You think the product mix may be going wrong? Think? May? You lack confidence to put up prices because you have no understanding of the criteria on which your customers buy. And if you haven't actually spoken to the bank manager yet and have no idea whether that market trend is important to your customers you need facts – fast.

KEY MESSAGE – Get the facts. All the facts. Facts are power. Facts will get you through this tough time.

What **ACTION** do you need to take? Capture it here...

2. Money facts

Here's what you need to know: your margin on each product, your product mix and the profitability per product line, profitability per salesperson, component costs, expenses, history of such information, forecast of such information pipeline of sales with risk ratings, salaries, expenses, the cost of your debts, your contractual terms with customers and suppliers. Only once you know these facts can you make informed decisions.

KEY MESSAGE – Know your money facts.

What **ACTION** do you need to take? Capture it here...

3. Direction facts

What is our strategy? What are our tactical campaigns? What do we need to be doing on a daily basis to ensure success? Who needs to be doing what?

KEY MESSAGE – Know your direction facts. And get them at action, milestone and accountability level.

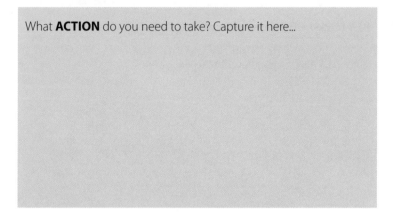

What **ACTION** do you need to take? Capture it here...

4. Customer facts

When was the last time you really talked to your customers about what they really, really want from you? How about inviting in a small group to talk to them?

KEY MESSAGE – Know your customer facts.

What **ACTION** do you need to take? Capture it here...

5. Team Motivation facts

This is an anxious time for the team. They are thinking, Will the company survive? Will I be made redundant? Will I be able to pay the mortgage? Decide over the next few weeks to spend time with as many of them one-to-one as appropriate and ask your management team to do the same with their people. Find out how people are coping with any anxieties. Find out if any of them have any flexibility such as the possibility of working shorter hours or taking an extended unpaid break should things come to that.

KEY MESSAGE – Get the facts on your team.

What **ACTION** do you need to take? Capture it here...

6. Bank facts

You no doubt keep all of this in a file somewhere. But do you *know* how much the bank charges you for everything and anything – standing orders, direct debits, foreign currency transactions? What's the deal with the current overdraft – could the bank call it in at any time? If you're not sure then find out, and once you know, you can try to get a better deal.

KEY MESSAGE – What are the facts about the bank?

What **ACTION** do you need to take? Capture it here...

7. Supplier facts

Talk to all of your suppliers. Reassure them about the relationship you wish to maintain. Check that you understand all of the contractual details, especially payment terms. See if there are any you can improve.

KEY MESSAGE – Get the facts on your suppliers.

What **ACTION** do you need to take? Capture it here...

8. Market facts

What are the trends in your market? What are coffee drinkers doing? Book readers? Cinema goers? Bank customers? Surfers of the net? Women? Men? Young adults? Someone, somewhere knows what's going on. This would be a great assignment for a student on placement from your local college so see what can be arranged. Be ahead of your competition in noticing market trends.

KEY MESSAGE – What are the facts about your market?

What **ACTION** do you need to take? Capture it here...

9. Economy facts

You'd be absolutely amazing if you knew to fact level what was going to happen in the economy. But you can check the daily indicators for your markets. Don't leave it to the experts; become your own expert.

KEY MESSAGE – What are the facts on the economy with relevance to your business?

What **ACTION** do you need to take? Capture it here...

10. Accountability facts

Who is responsible for any particular project, task or information? Are all the job descriptions up-to-date? If not, update them. Ensure everyone knows what his or her job fully entails and ask them to do it. Ask for accountability.

KEY MESSAGE – Get the facts that allow 100% accountability.

What **ACTION** do you need to take? Capture it here...

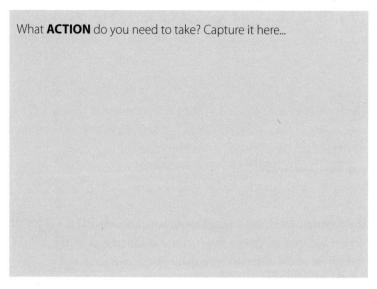

Facts are knowledge and knowledge is power. In tough times there is little leeway for a guess. Having the facts makes this unnecessary. Learn what you need to, then you can be confident about making the decisions that will steer your business out of and beyond this downturn.

3. Tough decisions

'I have no idea if we're in a recession or heading for one. Nor do I know where the market is going over the next few months. If I did, would I tell you for 35 cents? What I do know is that if you want to do well in the market, you've got to think ahead, not behind.'
Allan Sloan, **Washington Post**, 11 December 2007

● ●

The consensus is that the tough times have arrived, that it will hit all sectors and that it is going to get worse before it gets better. What's vital for all of us? The ability to make tough decisions and decide – rapidly – which ones to make. There's no time to lose.

WHAT DO YOU NEED TO DECIDE?
You need to make decisions and inevitably some of them will be tough. These might include decisions on: product lines which are losing you money, people who are not productive, customers who are difficult to work with, premises which are too expensive or which sector to give your resources to. No matter how tough these decisions are you must make them today. Here's how.

1. Scale up your decision making
Make decisions more quickly, more often and with a careful balance of short- and long-term consequences. Get a clear handle on your decision criteria: revenue, profit, market share, and so on. Business battles in hard times are won or lost by the ability to make clear decisions under pressure with insufficient data, and to be able to live with the consequences of those decisions with no early sign of success.

In other words, you need to have courage under fire. If you are confident that one part of your product line could take a price increase which would more than cover the reductions which are essential on other parts of the line, do it. There may be initial customer push back, but do it. The eventual profitability will be glorious – but it won't happen unless you can make tough decisions.

KEY MESSAGE – Start taking clear, visible decisions having weighed all the available options and data you have. Implement the decision fully and live by it until it has been tested.

What **ACTION** do you need to take? Capture it here...

2. Balance now and the future

The angst of this tough time in the economy will pull you into fight-or-flight thinking. Balance that evolutionary pull with some good leadership. Ensure that every short-term decision you make also takes account of the long-term impact. Many an organisation has laid off good people only to need to start recruiting them again in three months' time, at great expense and training cost, often without being able to replace some of the rising stars they lost. Be clear: any bold short-term decision (well done!) has a more subtle long-term impact. Think it through – you'll soon get really good at it. Your competitors are deciding for now and now only. This could be one of the many edges you develop over the competition.

KEY MESSAGE – When you make a decision for now think,
What does this mean for the future?

What **ACTION** do you need to take? Capture it here...

3. Make good tough decisions by taking time out

The ability to work very long days is both admirable and necessary in the coming months, but it's not so good for your greatest asset, the one which is really going to get you through this time: your brain. Look after it – give it a break. Go home early and watch a film. Take a walk in the park at lunchtime. Go to bed with a great novel. Start swimming. Start walking more. Brainstorm with your partner (in business, in life or in both). Buy a different marketing book and scan for ideas. Take your notebook to the cafe. Work hard, yes, but work smart, too. Sometimes you can do less and achieve more.

KEY MESSAGE – Look after what is your greatest asset by far in this recession: your brain. Take time out.

What **ACTION** do you need to take? Capture it here...

4. Make tough decisions on revenue and profit

Where will your revenue and profit really come from over the next nine to eighteen months? Draw up a matrix: products and/or services along the horizontal axis, customers and/or markets on the vertical. At the intersections start doing calculations. Get explicit. Sum rows and columns: where will the money come from? Is that money profitable money? As a consequence of your analysis make tough decisions on where you will spend your marketing budget, which markets/customers you will chase and which markets/customers you will let go. Get tough.

KEY MESSAGE – Make some tough decisions on where the (profitable) money is going to come from.

What **ACTION** do you need to take? Capture it here...

5. Combine the best of logic with the best of intuition

Make good tough decisions by using balance sheets plus heart and guts. You're going to be making a lot of tough decisions over the coming months. What's your methodology; your process? Consider this:

- **Stage 1** Get the facts ('We make no money on that product range').

- **Stage 2** What are your decision criteria ('Do we need a presence in that market')?

- **Stage 3** Draw up a balance sheet (pros and cons) and draw a conclusion.

- **Stage 4** Does the decision align with your gut feeling? If so implement it. If not be suspicious and review the data again.

KEY MESSAGE – Don't ignore your gut feelings when making tough decisions.

What **ACTION** do you need to take? Capture it here...

6. Make tough decisions about people

When you look at your prioritised cost spreadsheet, people will keep coming out on the top of that list. You'll need to make some tough decisions. The key questions to ask are, Is it simply their cost that stops me wanting to keep them? If it is performance too, can anything be done about that? If it is simply cost can anything be done – with their agreement – to moderate the cost for a short period? People who enjoy their jobs will want to keep them even if it requires some temporary hardship. If you have to let people go, do your utmost to maintain the relationships and to help them find new positions. Talk to your solicitor and gain ten minutes of advice on the procedure for redundancy; you don't want to be distracted by having fired someone in a way which breaks the law.

KEY MESSAGE – Do the best for your people whether they go or stay.

What **ACTION** do you need to take? Capture it here...

7. Make good tough decisions by talking to others

Talk to your network. Ask your contacts what they would do, and return the favour by helping them out. Tough decisions are harder to make on your own. A third party's insight, especially from somebody who is not emotionally involved, can be invaluable.

KEY MESSAGE – Build a support network.

What **ACTION** do you need to take? Capture it here...

8. Make tough decisions about your previous vanity, ego, foibles and history

This is a great time to break some patterns and silly practices. Some things are just that way because they always have been, but that attitude needs to be challenged as that is where a lot of cost is potentially hidden. Why are there two sites for the business, with the travel expenses and inevitable miscommunication this entails? Why are you paying over the odds for office space just to have a prestigious address? Why are there so many grades of company car? Has anyone ever validated the huge standing order that goes to the accountants? Why are certain people based at home?

KEY MESSAGE – Get a handle on every traditional practice and ritual and ask: why?

What **ACTION** do you need to take? Capture it here...

9. Make tough decisions throughout the business

This means everything – from major strategies to seemingly less significant items: pay reviews; bonuses; expenses; holidays; capital investment; which customers you should develop and which you need to let go; which suppliers you develop and which you switch; what you do about funding; how you should approach the bank; what you want your accountant to prepare for you; what you will say at the company annual meeting; how you will demonstrate that your attitude is 'we're in this together' not 'it's us and them'. Create a checklist on your whiteboard of tough decisions to be made. Start working through it.

KEY MESSAGE – Create your decision checklist.

What **ACTION** do you need to take? Capture it here...

10. A tough decision is not a decision until it is turned into an action

So you've decided to do more telephone cold calling? Excellent idea – so what's the action? Does a dedicated quiet room need to be set up? Is a list of names needed? Is a guideline pitch needed? Who's going to do those things, and when? Make a decision: take an immediate action. That's real, tough decision making.

KEY MESSAGE – A decision is not a decision until you've acted on it.

What **ACTION** do you need to take? Capture it here...

11. A complex tough decision is not a decision until it is turned into a plan

So you're going to enter a new, premium market? Excellent – so, what is your plan? Who is doing promotion ... messaging ... branding ... product specification ... training the sales teams ... creating documentation? Yes – you need a plan. And a plan has actions with milestones. It also identifies the critical path; the set of actions which if delayed puts the whole project at risk.

KEY MESSAGE – A complex decision is not a decision until you have created a plan and you know the critical path.

What **ACTION** do you need to take? Capture it here...

12. Create triggers to enable tough decision making

A trigger reminds you of decisions you need to make and points you need to review. Create timed triggers in your diary. Each week set triggers such as team review, production figures analysis and costs saved to date report. Set up daily triggers: 8 o'clock margin review, 11 o'clock production line review, and so on. Use your brain for thinking, use your computer for reminding.

> **KEY MESSAGE – Keep it simple** by setting up triggers to make tough decisions.

What **ACTION** do you need to take? Capture it here...

Be prepared to make some of the toughest decisions of your business career and be prepared to make them promptly. It'll absolutely, definitely be the difference that makes the difference.

4. People

'Fund managers across the world have turned "super-bearish" over the last month, abandoning hope that Europe and Asia can escape contagion from the US housing crisis. A Merrill Lynch survey found that a fifth of big investors now expect an outright global recession, an occurrence not seen since the 1930s.'
Daily Telegraph, online edition 17 January 2008

● ●

The consensus is that the tough times have arrived, that it will hit all sectors and that it is going to get worse before it gets better. What's on the critical path for success? People. Let's take a look at them.

PEOPLE POWER

You need to maintain morale and find ways to get more out of fewer people. You may well have to let some employees go. Make sure you hold on to the enthusiastic good people. You must maintain morale even when many of the carrots have gone. Here's how.

1. Communicate

There's a lot of worry among your people. They hear bad news on the TV. There's more in the free newspaper on the train. But the guy in the pub says there's nothing you can do about it anyway, so why worry? This is where you come in: a bit of decent focused quality communication is needed. If you don't already, start the routine of a monthly 'call out' or a briefing to the whole of the organisation. If, because of logistics or key roles, it is really not possible to do that, get your messages rolled out by team leaders on the same day you do your messaging. And what do you cover? Basic business facts: revenue this month, profit this month and sales forecast; market conditions; people issues – leavers and joiners. Allow questions, but always close on your up-beat summary. Tell it straight but focus on what is going well and keep any bad news in ordinary neutral language. People should come away thinking, 'this is a company which is doing its damnedest in tough times and I believe they will come through although it's not going to be easy'. Can you do that? Of course you can, and they will appreciate you for doing it.

KEY MESSAGE – Tell it straight. Tell it at least once a month.

What **ACTION** do you need to take? Capture it here...

2. Educate

This is a really good time to start some education. Perhaps you can do five minutes at each of your company call-outs (see above). For example, a lot of people unfortunately confuse revenue with profit. This means at the very least when they hear of a $2000/$20,000/

$2,000,000 deal they think all the company's problems are over. At worst they don't really appreciate how, especially when times are bad, every cent really does count.

> **KEY MESSAGE – Start the education process** and ask your team leaders to roll that process out through the organisation.

What **ACTION** do you need to take? Capture it here...

3. Motivate

You'll have problems if your people are not motivated. People who are not motivated rarely give of their best, tend to make more mistakes and often simply leave. Along the way they may become political and cause problems, so it's best to keep people motivated. How? Keep it simple, because it really is. Address the basics first. How can someone give of their best if they don't have a desk or a computer? If the office temperature is too high? If they don't know exactly what they are meant to be doing? So sort out the basics, or, in the case of the computer, explain why it can't be provided yet.

The other level of motivation is the higher level. Human beings are motivated by a wish to live the life they dream of. If you can help them realise that dream, whether they are a single mum who simply wants to work part-time or a keen young graduate who wants to excel at marketing, they will do their best for you. And if that seems a bit of luxury to be considering in tough times, think again – it's the best time.

KEY MESSAGE – Motivate all your people by addressing the basics and supporting their dreams.

What **ACTION** do you need to take? Capture it here...

4. Train

Training is a real win–win investment. Good training motivates and makes people work more effectively. Of course it costs money, so certainly delay what you can and buy more wisely. Discuss if a two-day course can be done in one. But keep good training going, for them and for you.

KEY MESSAGE – Keep training.

What **ACTION** do you need to take? Capture it here...

5. Coach

Right now you'll probably be attempting to do more with fewer people. One way to do that is to raise their skills level. Training makes a start, but coaching continues the process. Whether it is large account selling, purchasing, clearing cafe tables, proofreading or leading a team of graduate trainees, coach them how to do their job extraordinarily well.

KEY MESSAGE – Build on training with coaching.

What **ACTION** do you need to take? Capture it here...

6. Ask them to be brilliant at the basics

Remind them that more than ever, every possible interaction with the customer or potential customer counts. Ask all of your team to be brilliant at the basics: to answer the phone on time, be polite and helpful, check all work, be accurate, be loyal. Above all they ned to do all the small stuff which stacks up and can make the difference between winning business and not.

KEY MESSAGE – Get brilliant at the basics.

What **ACTION** do you need to take? Capture it here...

7. Get them to be team players

It's true that individuals are not as effective as a real team, but a group of people who are not working effectively together are a lot less productive than individuals. Ensure all groups become teams as quickly as possible. The biggest blocker to building an effective team is normally differences between people. Resolve those by encouraging discussion of working practices at team meetings; as soon as possible create an environment where people can articulate differences without it causing damage to the relationship.

KEY MESSAGE – Encourage differences to be managed rather than resented.

What **ACTION** do you need to take? Capture it here...

8. Watch the stress levels

A bit of stress is good for all of us. We all enjoy the buzz we get from a certain level of adrenaline. But too much stress stops people being effective and can of course lead to illness which, regardless of the consequences for the person concerned, doesn't help business productivity. Your behaviour will be followed so encourage people to work hard during office hours but then (apart from the odd crisis) go home and have a life outside work.

KEY MESSAGE – There is a life beyond work, enjoy it.

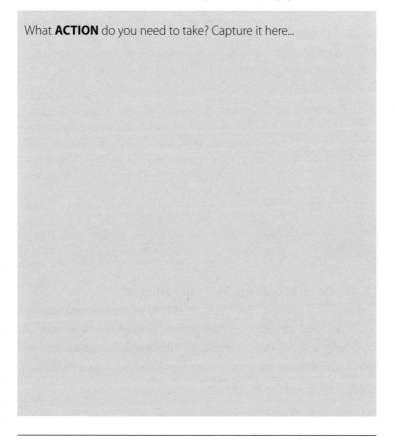

What **ACTION** do you need to take? Capture it here...

9. Celebrate success

Note all good news. Try to keep something up your sleeve for the monthly meeting. Try to have something significant every week. If a deal has been very rewarding for the business, thank everyone with something tangible which is appropriate to grades, experience and the industry in which you work. A bottle of wine or a gift voucher can go a long way in making people feel appreciated.

KEY MESSAGE – Note achievements and reward appropriately.

What **ACTION** do you need to take? Capture it here...

10. Recruit on knowledge, skills and attitude

You may be fortunate enough to be able to increase headcount. Or you may need to replace a key player. Remember to recruit on knowledge and skills and attitude. And in a tough market the attitude factor will be more important than ever. Can this person be flexible, a team player and resourceful?

KEY MESSAGE – Become a canny recruiter

What **ACTION** do you need to take? Capture it here...

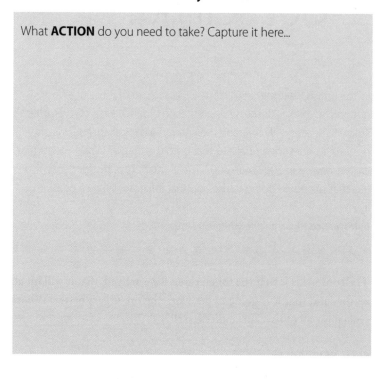

Act well and you can increase people productivity dramatically. It's easy to act well – get close to your people, be honest and lead by example. Start today.

5. Get selling!

'…the British Chamber of Commerce has found that the business outlook for 2008 is depressed and that confidence in the Government's ability to successfully manage the economy has collapsed. 75% of businesses questioned believe that both the UK and World economies will be weaker in 2008 than 2007. Three-quarters of respondents also feel that prices are going to rise and that inflation will be a problem in 2008.'

bytestart.co.uk on-line newsletter, 9 January 2008

● ●

The consensus is that the tough times have arrived, that it will hit all sectors and that it is going to get worse before it gets better. What's crucial for all of us? The ability to sell.

SELL, SELL, SELL

Start selling again, not just taking orders. Handle all the objections, especially price ones. Develop great accounts quickly and find quick wins. Negotiate to protect every bit of margin. You must revive the ancient art of selling, and sell your way out of this recession. Here's how.

1. Start selling again

Selling is something you **do**; a proactive process. Order taking is easy when it is busy, but depressing and business-breaking in a recession. Get your sales team selling and get everyone in the organisation sales focused. Selling is about turning prospects (people who might buy) into customers (people who have bought); customers into clients (people who buy a lot from you); clients into accounts (people who buy a lot from you and are loyal) and accounts into advocates (people who rave about you and say how wonderful you are). And it is dead easy. Why do you want to do it? Because (as you know) the cost (financial and emotional) of getting customers is very, very high. But once you have got them, assuming you look after them, the cost of sale goes down and profitability goes up. And we love that.

KEY MESSAGE – Start strategically and tactically turning prospects into customers into clients into accounts into advocates.

What **ACTION** do you need to take? Capture it here...

2. What's special about you?

Identify what is special about what you're offering. If you don't have anything, create something. If there is nothing special about you, you are effectively the same as the competition, and if you are the same as the competition you can only distinguish yourself on price, which of course means lower price. You don't want to reduce prices in any business climate, but especially not in a recession. So create difference, create specialness. This can come from your company ('local'), your product ('available in red') or you and your people ('astonishingly helpful'). The one you can change most quickly is that last one, of course. If you have great differences, make sure they are well communicated in your literature; simply because *you* are familiar with them don't assume they are obvious to the customer.

KEY MESSAGE – Company+product+you = difference.
Communicate that difference clearly.

What **ACTION** do you need to take? Capture it here...

3. Set sales goals carefully
Sales goals and targets are often simply revenue targets, generated by some spreadsheet in the bowels of the organisation. Difficulties arise when sales teams have the authority to discount – mix and margin projections fly out of the window. Consider seriously targeting the sales teams on margin and profit, or at the very least reward non-discounting.

KEY MESSAGE – Target what you really want, which is generally profit.

What **ACTION** do you need to take? Capture it here...

4. Don't talk price, talk value

There is no perfect price. Price is just a clue, shorthand that gives us guidance about value. This is an expensive car so it must be a great car; this is a cheap pen so I'm dubious about its quality. So don't talk price and let the customer get the wrong idea, talk value. Explain what it will do for them. Your product must have the answers to lots of their 'so what?' questions. In this coffee shop we recycle all the paper cups (so what?) so you know you are not damaging the environment. At this publisher we give you clear, bite-sized pieces of information (so what?) because we know you are keen to learn but also very busy. So get the sales team together and brainstorm the 'so what?' questions. Learn them and use them.

KEY MESSAGE – Talking price is a downward slope: talk value.

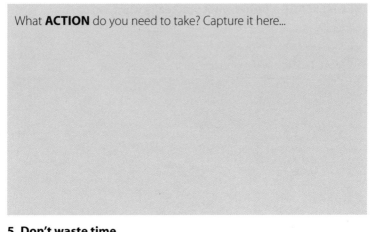

What **ACTION** do you need to take? Capture it here...

5. Don't waste time

If you are selling a small value commodity it is often just a numbers game. But where you are selling a solution, especially a high-price solution, don't waste your time. Qualify who you should be speaking to – you are looking for someone who could be a FAN of yours. In other words they have **F**unds, **A**uthority and a **N**eed for your product.

KEY MESSAGE – Only spend time talking with 'qualified' people.

What **ACTION** do you need to take? Capture it here...

6. Ask for the business

Asking for the business is not pushy, it is making it easy for the person to buy. Would you like to take this shirt? Which colour do you prefer? So, does our proposal seem attractive? Would you like a cake with your sandwich? If you were to double your order we could offer free shipping. Ask for the business, and keep asking for the business.

KEY MESSAGE – Ask and keep asking for the business.

What **ACTION** do you need to take? Capture it here...

7. Don't worry about customer concerns

When you ask people to buy, they naturally express concerns. Yes, buying double the volume would be useful but we have nowhere to store it. Isn't this a model which has been out for a while; won't it be replaced soon? I don't think we really need maintenance. These are concerns, but a concern is feedback; it tells you where to go next in the conversation. OK, let's think about how we can increase the volume and make it worthwhile to you even with your storage issue. Of course, there will undoubtedly be newer models, but this model now has an expansive range of support literature, which should be invaluable as you are new to photography. Get the team together and practise resolving these concerns.

KEY MESSAGE – A concern is not a problem, it's a signal that the person is serious.

What **ACTION** do you need to take? Capture it here...

8. You can't sell unless you know what they want

You certainly can't express your differences unless you know what they really want, so ask questions. Open questions such as, What are you trying to do here ... Why did you choose that strategy? Encourage people to talk. Open questions are great for building rapport and getting background information. Closed questions such as, How much money do you have? tend to encourage yes, no or one word answers. They are great for essential information, for qualifying and of course for getting final decisions. Become more conscious of your sales conversations and use the complementary nature of the two kinds of question.

KEY MESSAGE – Ask the right sort of questions at the right time.

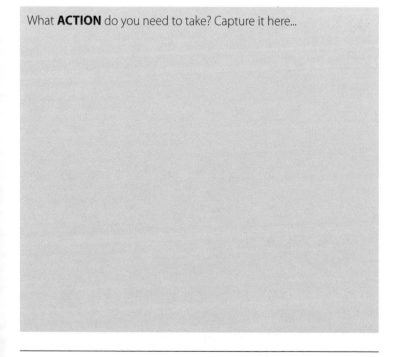

What **ACTION** do you need to take? Capture it here...

9. Have loads of potential business

There is nothing much worse than a quarter when you don't have enough business in the first place, and then deals collapse around you. Start by making sure you have loads of business; loads of prospects. Three underused methods are:

1. Asking everyone with whom you do business, Who else should I be talking to?

2. Building your network and staying in touch with everyone with whom you have done business.

3. Cold calling (see 10, below).

KEY MESSAGE – Have more potential business than you can handle.

What **ACTION** do you need to take? Capture it here...

10. Learn how to make cold calls

The key thing to remember is that, although it's going to be unpleasant at times, you can handle that, because you are looking forward to the wins. The amazing thing about telephone cold calling is you can choose the company you deal with. Identify who you want to be doing business with and ring them; of course they will not be delighted to hear from you but as long as they are talking, explain what's special about you. Don't sell the product, sell a meeting. Go on, try it, because everybody else is too frightened.

> **KEY MESSAGE – Cold calls may not be fun**, but the long-term business from them *is* fun.

What **ACTION** do you need to take? Capture it here...

11. Learn how to negotiate

You have found a company, asked questions, illustrated your uniqueness and done a pitch, and you are close to winning the business. But (surprise surprise) they want discount. Here are the essentials of negotiation:

- Don't negotiate until you have sold.

- Don't use discount as a route to selling.

- Don't give anything unless you get something in return, e.g. I could give 3.5% but I would need a formal order, today.

- Give small. If you have 15% up your sleeve, just give 3% then they will appreciate it when you eventually give 6%.

- Give slowly – it's about appreciation.

- Keep reminding them that whatever you agree rolls back to zero next financial year, otherwise they will start this year's agreement with last year's discount as their new base.

KEY MESSAGE – Simply discounting is not selling nor is it negotiation. Learn both skills.

What **ACTION** do you need to take? Capture it here...

12. Learn more about selling

Buy books on selling and read them. Get the sales team to read them and ask for insights to be shared at the sales meeting. Create mini role-plays at team sessions. Buy some audiobooks that those on the road can listen to before key meetings. Learn about selling.

KEY MESSAGE – Did we mention, learn about selling?

What **ACTION** do you need to take? Capture it here...

13. Love your accounts

Never, ever take a good account for granted. Never assume they don't have choice. Don't find them dull and chase new, exciting, challenging business. Love the accounts you have because they will help you sleep at night, they pay the bills and they are your references. Meet them, talk to them, look after them.

KEY MESSAGE – Love your accounts.

What **ACTION** do you need to take? Capture it here...

This is it. This is the one. Sell! It's a verb; it's about action. Get the sales team selling, get everyone who comes into contact with the customer selling. You can sell better than your competitors by giving this loads of attention. That's all it needs. Get to it.

6. Marketing

'The question for many economists is not if the US economy will fall into a recession. It's whether it already has. The formal recognition of a start of a recession probably wouldn't come for at least six months if not more than a year, as official judges from the National Bureau of Economic Research (NBER) pore through various economic readings. But top economists from two of the major Wall Street firms – Merrill Lynch and Goldman Sachs – say recession is likely already here.'
CNNMoney.com, 10 January 2008

● ●

The consensus is that the tough times have arrived, that it will hit all sectors and that it is going to get worse before it gets better. We need to return to our marketing skills.

REAL MARKETING
Now is the perfect time to do real marketing: targeting, segmenting, adding value at little cost. It's very tempting to reduce the marketing budget. This would be a mistake; just spend it much more wisely. Marketing is the key to your long-term future; remember this slump will end and you want to be ready. You must keep your marketing investment rolling. Here's how.

1. Start marketing again
Do you remember Kotler? Did you ever study him on your MBA or read about him in an in-flight magazine? Kotler came up with the '4Ps', an absolute bedrock of all marketing principles. Although they

have been repackaged many times (even by Kotler himself), the basics remain sound. Success in business is about the right combination of:

■ **Product**, sold through the right

■ **Place** (channel), at the right

■ **Price** with appropriate

■ **Promotion**.

Now, how simple is that? What these tough times do is to get us to go back to the core of our marketing thinking. And to do that you need to run an off-site meeting.

KEY MESSAGE – Return to your core marketing principles.

What **ACTION** do you need to take? Capture it here...

2. Run an off-site meeting?

You need to go off site because you have been so busy the last few years in a pleasantly heady economy that you have lost sight of the core of your business. If you stay in the office, the phone will ring and Andy from despatch will always need a signature. So you are going to get off site. But keep it cheap. Someone's kitchen will do fine. No phones or email. You need a few flip-charts, some masking tape and pens. Here are the three questions you are going to ask at that off-site meeting:

■ What business are we in now?

■ What business do we need to be in, in three years' time?

■ How can we close the gap?

For each of the time periods you will consider each of the 4Ps.

KEY MESSAGE – Invest in your success.

What **ACTION** do you need to take? Capture it here...

3. Product

Get clear on what you currently offer, whether it's a solid product (a desk, a book, a meal) or a service (car valeting or dry-cleaning) or a mixture of both. Get the flip-charts stuck up on the wall and identify current SWOTs:

■ **S**trengths (we have feature X; nobody else does).

■ **W**eaknesses (we do not offer 24–7 support and that is increasingly required).

■ **O**pportunities (in tough times we are leaner than most; we can probably grow at a greater rate than our competitors).

■ **T**hreats (we are only Australian based, many of our clients need us to have overseas offices).

Now identify some actions to take you to where you want to be in three years' time, knowing that at least nine months of that will be hard. Good work: you are managing the downturn but also using it as a stepping stone to greater things.

KEY MESSAGE – Analyse for success.

What **ACTION** do you need to take? Capture it here...

4. Price

Be provocative here: where did your current pricing policy come from? Is it history ('It's always been like this')? Cost plus some margin? The industry you are in? Copying the competition? It almost doesn't matter what the rationale is, as long as there is one. Because once you know it you can begin to experiment more scientifically, for instance by choosing some premium priced products to boost margin with little loss of share.

KEY MESSAGE – Get a pricing **strategy**.

What **ACTION** do you need to take? Capture it here...

5. Place

You must have a channel to your customers. You might sell direct, via a re-seller or both. Increasingly you have the internet too. Once again be provocative. How did the current channel structure originate? History? Market norms? Could you be radical and sell just through the internet, suddenly offer a highly personalised service or both?

KEY MESSAGE – How do you sell to your customers?

What **ACTION** do you need to take? Capture it here...

6. Promotion

This is classic marketing for the man in the street – advertising and PR. The key here is the increasing fragmentation of the market and the opportunity for more digital services such as online marketing; many of these are more exciting in that they give you more accountability for your spend.

KEY MESSAGE – Seek more accountability for your spend.

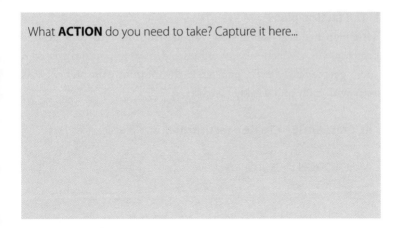

What **ACTION** do you need to take? Capture it here...

7. The strategic plan

Get one of the team to write this up. This is your analysis of where you are right now and where you want to be in three years' time. Set dates for your next strategic off-site meeting in twelve months' time. Now set quarterly dates for the tactical reviews which are your route to closing the gap.

> **KEY MESSAGE – Create a strategic plan** plus review dates.

What **ACTION** do you need to take? Capture it here...

8. The tactical plans

This plan needs to detail how you get from now to your desired future. It will have actions, milestones and, most importantly, owners, and it gets reviewed every quarter. In the meantime the owners walk away with daily and weekly task lists.

KEY MESSAGE – Create a tactical plan and practical task lists.

What **ACTION** do you need to take? Capture it here...

9. Marketing isn't (just)...

... mailshots, web sites, blogging, PR, cool clothes, using wifi in coffee bars, jargon, value chains, core competencies, Tom Peters, Saatchi & Saatchi, large lunch budgets and Moleskine notebooks.

KEY MESSAGE – Most marketing isn't what you think it is.

What **ACTION** do you need to take? Capture it here...

10. Marketing is...

... thinking, understanding, basics done really well, accountable budget spend, being different.

KEY MESSAGE – Marketing is art; but it's also science.

What **ACTION** do you need to take? Capture it here...

11. Budget marketing communications

Out of your strategic plan has come the need to communicate. A new web site perhaps, a blog, or just some cheap and cheerful postcards to send to key clients to remind them of what you are up to these days? But a lot of this involves expenditure, so be creative and resourceful. Ask at local colleges and universities for students who want real experience or designers who want to expand their portfolios. Doing a day's work for you at budget prices beats clearing tables and strengthens their CV. Make calls and interview a few. You may even find a great enthusiastic marketeer who can join you when this period is over and they have graduated. It is a possibility.

KEY MESSAGE – Get quality work from budget sources. It's a win–win situation.

What **ACTION** do you need to take? Capture it here...

12. Budget strategic marketing

You're probably feeling you'd like a bit of advice on some of your final analysis – a sort of sounding board. It's a great idea but where do you go? Well, start at your local college again. Lecturers working in those fields have an insatiable desire for case studies: that's where you come in. Even if you have to pay for some of the advice, it should be a lot cheaper and more flexible than major consultancy day rates.

KEY MESSAGE – Get an expert's review of your thinking.

What **ACTION** do you need to take? Capture it here...

13. Love marketing

Decide to learn a lot more about marketing. Decide that this recession will cause you to review where your business is and where you want to take it. Decide to (re-)learn the basics of marketing and apply them. Decide to have a strategy and to ensure it is lived and breathed throughout your business on a daily basis.

KEY MESSAGE – Love marketing: it's really useful.

What **ACTION** do you need to take? Capture it here...

As you have (re-)realised, real marketing, especially in a recession, is not a luxury. Get back to the 4Ps, start thinking again and don't think a distinct strategy is beyond you; it needs to be a part of you.

7. Back to basics

'During good economic times, companies succeed despite their weaknesses. But during bad economic times, they struggle because of them.'
Paul Kosakowski

● ●

The consensus is that the tough times have arrived, that it will hit all sectors and that it is going to get worse before it gets better. So it's essential we get brilliant at the basics.

REVIEW THE BASICS

The basics include answering the phone, sending an invoice, shipping a parcel, personal attitude. Make money and save money with the everyday simple no-brainer (but oh-so-easily-forgotten) stuff. Here's how.

1. Are you brilliant at the basics?

What happens when someone arrives at your offices, your factory or even your houseboat turned office? Can they find you? Can they park easily or are all the car-parking spots occupied by the sales team (who by the way ought to be out on the road)? Is reception welcoming or is that poor temp attempting to pack a box for courier collection and send a fax while giving your visitor a security badge? Is there a fresh newspaper or has that been one of your cutbacks? Is their host on time? Is he/she upbeat, or complaining about this recession? Is the meeting room partly a storeroom with boxes and trailing wires from the video-conference machine? Is the coffee an apology? Have the corporate brochures run out? Are there towels in the wash-rooms? It's all basic stuff but so easy to neglect. Make a 'mystery shopper' visit to your place. Ring in, visit, try to park, try to order. Detail an action list and act on it. It's a low budget way of making a huge difference.

KEY MESSAGE – Identify the basic standards for your organisation and get brilliant at them.

What **ACTION** do you need to take? Capture it here...

2. Promote what you do all the time, every time

Take a look at the bottom of one of your emails. No doubt there's some legal stuff, probably some telephone numbers. But does it sell for you? Does it tell the person who receives that email about everything you do and how they can find more information? No, because they know you – you think. They don't actually – customers are surprisingly blinkered; they buy one thing and then go elsewhere for something else which is actually in one of your product ranges that they don't even know about. Put a snappy buyline on the bottom of your email and have a link to your web site. Change those end of email promotions regularly. Have interesting PR snippets on the wall in reception. Display your products. Use the back of your business cards to explain what you do and/or why you are special. Not just The Wizard Cafe (on the front), but (on the back) 'We cook the best sausages in town: join us any morning from 6.30 for a great Aussie breakfast'. Take every opportunity to sell the sizzle.

KEY MESSAGE – Get the basics of self-promotion happening at every opportunity.

What **ACTION** do you need to take? Capture it here...

3. Who's tracking the money?

Who gets the cheques into the bank account immediately? Lunchtime would do nicely – yes I know there's a queue, but it's also reducing our overdraft. Is there a carefully managed purchase order system? Are there expenses guidelines? Are expenses submitted regularly, checked and if necessary queried? Are invoices sent immediately? Are they checked to ensure they won't be returned because of a silly mistake? Are they sent out first class? Are there departmental budgets, and who monitors them? Ask your bank's business adviser how she would save money in your business without spending more money with the bank. Have you sorted on-line banking so you can manage your account(s) and further reduce charges?

KEY MESSAGE – Get the basics of money management sorted.

What **ACTION** do you need to take? Capture it here...

4. What does your web site say to the world?

You know very well it's a busy, busy world out there. More so in recessionary times, and in times of financial hardship people are often a little stressed as well. So, once they have decided to find out about you by looking at your site, is it a straightforward experience or do they have to wait for a clutter of clever graphics to load? Can they find your phone number in seconds? ... An overview of your products? ... An address if they want to send you something? Make it easy to deal with you – even in the most traditional of businesses, your web site is increasingly how you are viewed. Check that everything, especially prices if revealed, is up-to-date and that you are being analysed properly on comparison tables.

KEY MESSAGE – Create a brilliantly simple and basic web site.

What **ACTION** do you need to take? Capture it here...

5. Be resourceful!

Let's avoid the term 'positive thinking' here; after all things aren't always that positive if you are chasing cash and a good client has just gone bust. But do be resourceful, use resourceful language and don't reveal your problems to the world. If clients ask you how business is simply say 'good, though challenging'. They want your confidence, not your worries. Ask all team leaders in your organisation to talk up success and keep problems in perspective.

KEY MESSAGE – Maintain a positive appearance

What **ACTION** do you need to take? Capture it here...

6. What can you outsource, and hence reinvent?

Small or large, you have specialist activities in your business which may well be worth outsourcing. You know that the cost of a person is not just their salary and associated taxes; it's also their share of the overheads. But a cost an accountant can't factor in is an employee's lack of flexibility. Outsourcing and contractors may well give you the flexibility you need for the future. This calls for a real back-to-basics attitude in the way you structure your business. Here's the power question: if you were redesigning your business from scratch today, how would you do it? Now, seriously consider doing that.

KEY MESSAGE – Reinvent your business.

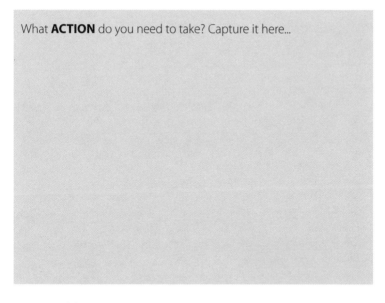

What **ACTION** do you need to take? Capture it here...

7. Start a blog

People always like to know who they are buying from. During tricky financial periods they really like to know they can trust the organisation they are dealing with. A blog is a great way of doing that: it reveals your personality directly; it talks to the world. It is instantly responsive. A blog costs close to nothing to run bar your time. And with a bit of patience and nurturing you can develop a wide readership; possibly in your market you can be one of the first to decide to start blogging and get ahead of the curve. Remember an absolute basic of selling is: 'people buy people'. This is a cool way to do it using technology. Get on the net and search on blogs in your field. You'll soon learn what it's all about.

KEY MESSAGE – An absolute basic is that people buy people: a blog displays your personality to the world at large.

What **ACTION** do you need to take? Capture it here...

8. Less they, more I/we

Encourage and display responsibility and accountability in these lean times. There is no fat for excuses. If regular accounts are not buying from you, find some others. If you're late (again) because of the traffic, find another route or get up earlier or both. If you miss the post at the local postbox walk across town to the main post office. Encourage a culture where people do what is necessary to help the company come out of this stronger than when it went in. More, 'I/we will make this happen' and a lot less, 'This isn't fair'.

KEY MESSAGE – Take ownership – don't say, 'My boss wouldn't let me'.

What **ACTION** do you need to take? Capture it here...

9. Look after yourself: be the best version of you.

Whether you are leading others or just leading yourself you need to be on top form most of the time. Others will be looking to you for guidance and a sense that it'll be OK. You need to be thinking clearly, you need great focus and you need energy resources. Look after yourself. Get sleep, and ensure you sleep well (avoid late-night work, especially email, wind down several hours before sleep). Get exercise (not the stuff which injures; the stuff which makes you feel better). Keep hydrated. Carry a notebook to focus on actions that need to be taken and record flashes of insight. Enjoy your weekends and take your holidays.

KEY MESSAGE – There is nothing more basic than remembering to look after yourself.

What **ACTION** do you need to take? Capture it here...

Brilliant at the basics is a heck of a differentiator in itself. Get it supporting a distinct strategy and you have got a real winner. Get someone addressing those basics now.

8. Communicate

'Oil fell the past three days because of a growing conviction that the U.S., which consumes 25 per cent of the world's oil, is already in a recession. U.S. equities plunged yesterday, capping their worst three-day decline since 2002.'
Bloomberg.com, 18 January 2008

● ●

The consensus is that the tough times have arrived, that it will hit all sectors and that it is going to get worse before it gets better. You'll need to be a first class communicator; from the junior in the post room to the chief executive, with your clients and with your suppliers. You need to be able to tell it as it is and keep everybody confident.

COMMUNICATE TO ACCUMULATE

Talk to the staff, talk to the bank, talk to your customers. Get their help rather than their politics, irritation or even anger. You must start talking, informing and engaging all who can help you win in this slump. Here's how.

1. The quality of your communication has a huge impact on your success

The bottom line is that you are only as good as the quality of your communication. And that means, to everybody: the shareholders, the team, your clients and your suppliers. How do you talk to them? What message(s) do they pick up, explicitly and subliminally? Do they sense a company that is in control, or one on the rocks? Is the bank manager less concerned about your apparently very positive Excel spreadsheet than with the fact that the factory seems very quiet for this time of year. Become an even better communicator.

KEY MESSAGE – The quality of your communication will affect your success in these tough times.

What **ACTION** do you need to take? Capture it here...

2. Good communication is keeping everyone fully informed

Let people know what is going on – in troubled financial times, no news is definitely not good news. Tell your supplier why you haven't sent the cheque although it was due yesterday. Explain the problems you are having and that you have sent 60% of the amount today and the remainder will arrive on Monday. Apologise and say that you do not expect them to be your bankers and you'll be more on top of things in the future. Tell all your customers what you are doing. Have an immediate company-wide meeting to quash rumours, hyperbole and general politics. It's remarkable how resilient people are as long as they feel they are kept in the loop.

KEY MESSAGE – Keep everybody informed.

What **ACTION** do you need to take? Capture it here...

3. Good communication is investing in relationships

You need real trust from your team, clients, suppliers and the bank at the very least. You need to reduce their anxieties. Do that by investing in the relationship: basics such as doing what you say you are going to do, when you said you would. By being polite, by being loyal. You damage relationships by letting people down, or by talking behind their backs. Develop a great reputation as an excellent company to do business with. In times of business difficulty, basic qualities such as trust and accountability become highly valued and they are all reinforced (or not) by the quality of your communication. The really good news is that they are easy. Model the behaviours in your own organisation, remind people that those behaviours are important and when you catch people doing them thank them.

KEY MESSAGE – Invest in relationships and develop trust.

What **ACTION** do you need to take? Capture it here...

4. Good communication is assertive

Avoid conflict and adversarial conversations at all cost, though that does not mean you should not address issues which need sorting and resolving. Apart from being bad for your health, and potentially ruining your day, conflict is not good for business. Decide to be assertive. When you are assertive you respect and attempt to manage both points of view, 'So, you are looking for another two points of discount, while we are looking for more of your business; let's talk this through some more.' An assertive conversation is one in which whatever happens, even if you agree to disagree, the relationship is maintained, 'Let's leave it at that and speak again in a couple of days. We'd love to do business with you but the current proposal is simply not financially viable.' When you are passive it means you do not tackle the issue, 'OK, I guess the traffic is often bad on that route just try not to be any later than you are.' An aggressive person attempts to get his own way with no regard for others, 'Take it or leave it – you'll be stuffed if you don't work with us.' Assertive is firm but friendly, and straight-talking. People will enjoy dealing with you.

KEY MESSAGE – Be assertive.

What **ACTION** do you need to take? Capture it here...

5. A great presentation is not (just) a PowerPoint slide deck

You'll be giving presentations regularly, you'll be doing sales pitches, you'll be presenting to the bank for extended facilities and to your organisation at the regular monthly update. Seize every opportunity to present: it allows you to maintain control, get your messages across and keep to the point. But – and it's a big but – PowerPoint presentations have become the norm in business and they do not necessarily communicate that well. That's not a software problem, it's a user problem. Here's a structure for your next presentation which should improve the impact tenfold.

■ Start with a wow, something to grab their attention. This is particularly important in a sales pitch: go straight for an immediate benefit;

■ Do the agenda;

■ Talk about them (how you can help their business);

■ Talk about you (your solutions);

■ Take questions;

■ Summarise.

This sequence means that you have the last word. Finally, you need to ask for an action. If it's a sales pitch, ask for the business. If it's a company-wide meeting, ask people to do something differently (e.g. manage the detail). If it's with the bank manager ask if he will support that request for facilities extension. Only use slides to augment or illustrate: not as your script or teleprompter.

KEY MESSAGE – Communicate, don't just present slides.

What **ACTION** do you need to take? Capture it here...

6. Tell stories

A budget way to communicate your product is to create a great story around it, perhaps a client story, for example. Stories are easily transmittable, by word of mouth, and they're memorable. Slides full of bullet points are not. Turn your product benefits into great stories and make sure everybody knows and repeats them.

KEY MESSAGE – Become a storyteller.

What **ACTION** do you need to take? Capture it here...

7. Communicate simply and effectively

Pick up the phone more often; you'll get voicemail, but the nuances of your points and the warmth of your tone will come across as they never can in an email. Have a stack of postcards and drop personal notes of thanks. That's real communication.

KEY MESSAGE – Keep your communication real and simple.

What **ACTION** do you need to take? Capture it here...

8. Leadership is a decision, not a job title

Great leadership is about great communication. Now, more than ever, your organisation, be it of five or fifty or five thousand people, will need clear, encouraging communication. Remember that the title team leader, account manager or even CEO means nothing until you can give direction and inspire. That's a combination of words plus *wow*. Choose your words carefully. What's the change you want to see in people? What's the action you want them to take? Be clear, be explicit and be relevant. 'Wow' is the energy and momentum you put into it. If you want people to be inspired, you need to be inspiring; if you want people to be energised you need to be energising. Give them words plus wow and you'll give them great leadership.

KEY MESSAGE – Leadership is a decision: decide today.

What **ACTION** do you need to take? Capture it here...

9. Use excellent communication to get the best from difference

In too many organisations, differences cause problems: politics, game-playing and sometimes downright unpleasantness. These differences might be between departments ('Oh, that's those idiots in accounts for you') or between grades ('You're the newest so that's a job for you, I think'). That's crazy at any time, but when you need everybody working at their best and in fully functioning teams it's pure madness. Encourage clear, positive and open communication. Model such behaviours from the very top of the organisation. By respecting and valuing differences you can generate and capture excellent ideas, improve morale, boost productivity and have fun. All worth doing, you will agree.

KEY MESSAGE – Through great communication make a virtue of difference.

What **ACTION** do you need to take? Capture it here...

Start great communication today. You can't be the lone hero turning the organisation around, nor can you be the too-busy CEO. Tell people (customers, suppliers, employees) what's going on. Then they can work with you. It really is a team effort.

9. Opportunities

'California and Florida, two of the most important states in the US, are either in recession or on the brink of it, many economists now believe. The two states together account for nearly two-fifths of US gross domestic product. California alone would rank among the world's top 10 economies, while Florida would rank in the top 20.'
FT.com, 17 January 2008

● ●

The consensus is that the tough times have arrived, that it will hit all sectors and that it is going to get worse before it gets better. Better get focused then; better seize those opportunities. Let's get to work straight away.

SEIZING OPPORTUNITIES

Which of your competitors are faltering? How can you refocus, leave a market or enter a new market? Which accounts need your help? Which costs is it now the perfect time to let go of? You must grab opportunities now which will make you even stronger after the recession. Here's how.

1. A real opportunity

We human beings are funny in so many ways. But one thing is for sure, there's nothing quite like a common goal (especially a tough one) to get us really focused and, with a bit of good leadership, get us really performing, too. So, here's your common goal: surviving the downturn, the recession, the threat of our livelihoods being taken.

This business situation is a real opportunity to do the stuff you know has been needed for over a year now. It's time to get more focused, get leaner and maybe even get a bit meaner. Let's not be glib, but it really could be good news. So take that opportunity.

> **KEY MESSAGE – Think,** how can I get the best out of this opportunity?

What **ACTION** do you need to take? Capture it here...

2. A chance to really focus

Decide to decide. Decide to make the main thing, the main thing. You've probably been in business long enough now to know what you are really good at. Even if you have just started you *believe* you know what you are good at. Get back to it. Stop being distracted, determine your unique selling points and start selling them. Create a brilliant support team. Get the lab developing something cool. Say yes to what you're here for and politely say no to the rest. Focus maximises return, energises everybody and allows measurability. No focus means poor return, a demoralised workforce and poor metrics. Get focused today.

KEY MESSAGE – Focus on what is important to you.

What **ACTION** do you need to take? Capture it here...

3. A chance to reinvent

This downturn is the sharp end of changing global markets. It means that what you used to do, even when you come out of these hard times, will no longer be good enough: you'll need to reinvent. This is a chance to do it. Whether it is a gradual process, or whether you effectively close down the company and start again you'll need to reinvent. What you used to do well will no longer work.

KEY MESSAGE – Take the opportunity to change what your company does.

What **ACTION** do you need to take? Capture it here...

4. A chance to grow

Even though times are tough it is worth thinking big. Customers will be buying even more carefully; they'll be more discerning with their hard-pressed budgets. Of course they'll have a strong focus on price but you'll sell well and convince them that it's more than just that. Some of your competitors will cut costs in the wrong places. They won't have the support or account management infrastructure in place, they will let their customers down and budget pricing will be insufficient recompense. This is a real opportunity for you to take some of their accounts. Stay determined, maintain quality and sell rather than just taking orders. It's a really good opportunity to grow.

KEY MESSAGE – Decide to grow but in the way you really want. Revenue? Profit? More market share? Prestige? Whatever – make sure it's *your* growth.

What **ACTION** do you need to take? Capture it here...

5. Did success seduce you?

What is your core business? Where do you make your money? What are your people good at? Are you local or global? Are you big, small or medium? Are you direct or indirect? Are you basically you? Do you know what you do and what you are about or has success taken you down some routes which now seem difficult to maintain or unattractive? Everyone will understand if you now begin to resist the temptation to carry on regardless, and get back to what you are good at.

KEY MESSAGE – What are you good at? Make that your main thing.

What **ACTION** do you need to take? Capture it here...

6. A chance to recognise talent

There are one or two people in your team or in your organisation who are really good but have been held back to date because there haven't really been the opportunities. Now here is a chance. As part of your restructuring give them a temporary project: more responsibility, more decision making. Let them know there'll be no more money until the end of this period but encourage them to go for it and impress you anyway.

KEY MESSAGE – Spot and develop new talent.

What **ACTION** do you need to take? Capture it here...

7. A chance to be honest

There are one or two people in your team or in your organisation who haven't been performing. This is a chance to give them some clear goals and ask them to now deliver their very best. Otherwise, they need to be reminded, the organisation cannot carry them any longer. Ask your human resources people how you need to approach those conversations or get some employment law guidance from your solicitor.

KEY MESSAGE – Take the chance to be up-front with those who are not performing.

What **ACTION** do you need to take? Capture it here...

8. An opportunity to freshen up

Here's a great opportunity to tidy up the office, redecorate with budget paints, refile or discard obsolete paperwork, get some decent office cleaners, install some new lights, fix stuff which was broken and irritating, clean the whiteboard so daily figures can be displayed, start a library by asking people to bring in their best business books. Yes, it is cosmetic, but it works.

KEY MESSAGE – Seemingly superficial changes can make a difference.

What **ACTION** do you need to take? Capture it here...

9. A chance to lighten the load

There are too many costs which until now have just been absorbed. These need to go: the offsite storage, the overgenerous expense policy, the incentive scheme with too much focus on revenue and too little on margin.

KEY MESSAGE – Get a handle on the 'niggling' costs and distractions and get rid of them.

What **ACTION** do you need to take? Capture it here...

10. A chance to be radical

Now may be a perfect time to think about a short-term partnership which might become a long-term strategic partnership with someone. Who could complement your markets and products? Who could follow what you do? On whose business could you piggyback? There is a potential partner who would mean lower cost of sale, more account opportunities and access to extra resources if they and you can be open-minded enough. Maybe you want to go even further and merge to achieve more presence or credibility in the market, or maybe you want to sell up and get out. That wouldn't mean defeat or failure – as long as it is thought through it's a good strategic decision. What you have created to date will be keenly acquired by someone. That really does give you an opportunity to reinvent from the ground up.

KEY MESSAGE – Decide to be bold, to be radical.

What **ACTION** do you need to take? Capture it here...

Spot opportunities. It's not clichéd to say hard times expose opportunities which in headier times you might not be able to grasp. But you need to take your head out of the figures and/or the packing cases. Stay alert.

10. Time

'Slow growth in Japanese bank loans has added to concerns that the world's second-biggest economy may follow the US into possible recession.'
BBC News on bbc.co.uk, 11 January 2008

● ●

The consensus is that the tough times have arrived, that it will hit all sectors and that it is going to get worse before it gets better. We are going to need time to get out of this mess and yet time seems to be the last thing you have.

MAKING TIME

Focus, focus, focus. Tough times must not mean panic. It means balancing action time and investment time carefully. You must balance 'in' time and 'on' time. Here's how.

1. Understand time

More than ever, when times are tough it is crucial to understand that there are essentially two kinds of time which revolve around the two oft-quoted metrics of important and urgent. 'Important' we will define as anything which is addressing a goal: getting cash in, closing a profitable deal, creating a strategy plan for the next three years. 'Urgent' we'll define as anything which we need now: extension of the overdraft for three days to cover this mini cash-flow crisis, sending a fax to a possible new client who needs a total price list on our product. The time most businesses focus on, particularly in tough business times, is important and urgent: get the cash in the bank, close the deal this week. But stuff which is important and non-urgent such as the strategy plan or sales training tends to get delayed. Don't use the term non-urgent, use the term 'investing' and then it should make a lot more sense. Clearly the offsite meeting is not urgent but it is investing. Taking a walk at lunchtime is not urgent, but it is investing. Important and urgent is *in* time, when you are working *in* your business. Important and investing is when you are working *on* your business. To survive and thrive you need a careful blend of the two.

KEY MESSAGE – Mix *in* and *on* time for success.

What **ACTION** do you need to take? Capture it here...

2. Identify your *on* time and schedule it

Your 'in' time will always happen because of the urgency factor. And in challenging times it will have a little stress and adrenaline thrown in as well. As you walk into the office at ten to eight and start clearing email, you will be sucked into an 'in' day. It's not a bad kind of day, but it's a fire-fighting day, a surviving day; it's not a thriving kind of day. Take your schedule and block out some *on* time. Time you will preserve at all cost. To invest, to improve, to step beyond the day-to-day stuff. It will of course depend on your role but here are some suggestions:

- 15 minutes at the start of the day where you take stock, scan the strategic plan and think beyond the day-to-day pressures.

- 30 minutes at lunchtime where you get out, take a walk and think.

- 15 minutes at the end of the day where you review success and note key points for later in the week or month.

Schedule further sessions during the week for planning and team meetings. When they appear people will resist but remind them they are investing to make things easier in the future.

KEY MESSAGE – Invest for future success.

What **ACTION** do you need to take? Capture it here...

3. Stay focused

Have these documents close to you at all times: your strategy plan, your tactical plan and your task list (see Chapter 6, Marketing). Do not allow the addictive nature of today's crises to pull you too far from those previously agreed success plans. At least once a week review the strategy plan. At least twice a week review the tactical plan. And each day work on your task list ensuring that it is an appropriate balance of 'in' and 'on' time. Take breaks to ensure your mind and thinking stay fresh.

KEY MESSAGE – Avoid distraction and stick to the plan.

What **ACTION** do you need to take? Capture it here...

4. Run better meetings

Don't attend or run a meeting unless it has a clear goal. This goal should be on the whiteboard in front of everyone. Make sure all your meetings have an agenda to keep people on track. Delegate someone to note down actions, each of which should have an owner and a delivery date. Start and finish on time. Invite the smallest number of people possible.

KEY MESSAGE – Make your meetings efficient and targeted.

What **ACTION** do you need to take? Capture it here...

5. Practise kaizen: plan, do, review

As you know, 'kaizen' is constant, continual improvement. A simple model for doing that is to move from being simply a 'do' organisation to one which also plans and reviews. Plan the product launch, do the product launch and then review the product launch.

KEY MESSAGE – Plan, act and review for constant improvement.

What **ACTION** do you need to take? Capture it here...

6. Don't just react, make a choice

You will never have enough time to do all that could be done. Accept that. Decide to choose what needs to be done, not simply react. Make that choice by analysis of pay-off and benefit to the organisation. Don't just choose what is easy, what's attractive, who is shouting loudest or what will give you a quick win. Be proactive rather than reactive.

KEY MESSAGE – Choose by pay-off.

What **ACTION** do you need to take? Capture it here...

7. Choose by pay-off not just level of crisis

'By pay-off' means weighing the outcome of what you are doing against your strategic and tactical goals. If you constantly reference your well thought through plans and act in alignment with them, you will reach the higher ground you are seeking. But if you simply react to this minute's problem you'll get deeper into the mire. Make that choice.

KEY MESSAGE – Know your pay-off measures.

What **ACTION** do you need to take? Capture it here...

8. Get good at project management

Big stuff (e.g. breaking into a new market) tends not to happen as quickly as it should because it is mentally too hard (where do you start?) and difficult to find time. Follow basic project management principles and break it down into smaller and smaller chunks until the tasks become both time and brain friendly. Then get them assigned by owner and delivery date. Before you know where you are you will have both the new product and the new markets identified.

KEY MESSAGE – Break down tasks into manageable chunks and assign ownership.

What **ACTION** do you need to take? Capture it here...

9. Identify and reduce distractions

Your greatest asset is your brain and yet in this world of constant interruptions it's difficult to allow it to do its best for us at times. Eliminate distractions as much as you can. Batch process email, in other words check it and then forget it. Whether you do that once an hour or twice a day is up to you, but for a lot of us it has now become too intrusive. Switch it off, turn away and get on with the main job of writing that proposal. Let your team know there is a part of the day when you are not to be disturbed. Let reception know that there is a part of the day when they should take messages for you. Allow your brain to do its best by reducing the trivia.

KEY MESSAGE – Focus on the vital few, not the trivial many.

What **ACTION** do you need to take? Capture it here...

10. Use time to make you smarter

You have three potential intelligences. Firstly your neural intelligence, which is the collection of synaptic pathways sometimes measured by your IQ. There's not a lot you can do to improve that: it's genetic. Secondly you have your experiential intelligence. Perhaps you have been through tough times before, in which case you are pretty smart about a lot of ways to handle it. Lastly there is reflective intelligence, the one where you stop and think. This is the intelligence in play when out of nowhere you get ideas and problems get solved. That's why you need your 'on' time: sometimes you need to do less to achieve more.

KEY MESSAGE – Do less, achieve more.

What **ACTION** do you need to take? Capture it here…

You'll need a lot of 'in' time when you respond, react and wheel and deal. But it is vital that you have some 'on' time to develop, reposition and think. The quickest win with 'on' time is implementation of ideas from this blueprint.

11. Fun!

'In the *Telegraph* last week – David Owen, chief European economist at Dresdner Kleinwort Investment Bank, gave the odds of a recession in the UK during 2008 at 50%.'
Nadeem Walayat, **FXSTREET.com**, 24 December 2007

● ●

The consensus is that the tough times have arrived, that it will hit all sectors and that it is going to get worse before it gets better. How will you get through it all? Work hard, be focused, be creative and yes, have a bit of fun.

WHAT DO YOU MEAN – FUN?
Yes, it's going to be a long-haul, but you also need to ensure you are having some fun. It need not be expensive. Show people you value them and take time to re-energise them. You must have some fun otherwise what's the point? Here's how.

1. Are you serious about fun?
You need to take fun seriously. What's the point of any of this if, ultimately, you are not enjoying yourself? By all means, put in the long days, perhaps even the occasional all-nighter. Drive all the way up the motorway for a 7.30 breakfast meeting and then drive back with only a vague promise of business. Trade in your car for something a lot smaller. Move to serviced offices. Cope with being badly treated by one of your main suppliers. But all this will be a heck of a lot easier if there is some fun along the way. Having fun means that deep down you know it's all worthwhile, there are good bits to the day and at

times it's really good. Even in the toughest of times, you must feel it's all got a point and will work out in the end. If not you need to get out and do something else!

KEY MESSAGE – Think, expect and create fun.

What **ACTION** do you need to take? Capture it here...

2. Fun is valuing everyone for their contribution

Ensure everybody in your organisation, no matter how few or many of them there are, feels valued, is contributing to the overall effort and is having their own bit of fun each day. If you don't feel you can value someone, give them some clear feedback on what they need to be doing differently. It's no fun at all knowing you're not really valued and that you might be the next to go.

KEY MESSAGE – Value everyone. Allow everyone to contribute and have their bit of fun.

What **ACTION** do you need to take? Capture it here...

3. Fun is the occasional (budget) treat

The call is finished. Well done, not only did you get the deal, you only gave two points of discount and had budgeted for seven. A lot of people worked hard for that deal. It's a scorching day and although the air-conditioning is sort of working, you know what would be really nice? Ice creams all round. Do it!

KEY MESSAGE – Fun is a treat.

What **ACTION** do you need to take? Capture it here...

4. Fun is your family and friends

You love your work, but you need to take breaks from it. Watch a film, cook a special meal, go to the park with the kids, visit the museum. Forget it all for a while and have some fun. It'll make it a whole lot easier to look at those figures again tomorrow.

KEY MESSAGE – Switch off: really switch off.

What **ACTION** do you need to take? Capture it here...

5. Fun is a stand-up spot at the monthly meeting

Hang onto a great joke or anecdote for the company meeting. Ask your team leads for anything, especially if it's relevant to the business. Nothing which makes unpleasant fun of staff or customers though. Tell the joke just before your upbeat summary. You'll leave them feeling really good.

KEY MESSAGE – Let them leave feeling really good.

What **ACTION** do you need to take? Capture it here...

6. Fun is...

▦ Defusing tension in a difficult negotiation by being appropriately light-hearted, 'Hang on guys we are only talking about a shipment of plastic garden tables here'.

▦ Running each morning with a few other enthusiasts from work.

▦ Getting someone to come in and do bargain-rate shoulder massages one day as a treat that introduces her local business.

■ A cheap second-hand table-football machine in the corner of the canteen.

■ Inclusive. Still listening to music. Still reading. Still going out. Walking. Chilling. Being with great friends. Booking a cheap weekend to the coast.

KEY MESSAGE – Fun needn't cost the earth or take much effort.

What **ACTION** do you need to take? Capture it here...

7. Fun is not...

■ Wasting time by circulating joke emails, however funny.

■ Slowing people down in their jobs.

■ Teasing or bullying staff.

■ Just going down the pub and drinking.

■ Exclusive or cliquey.

KEY MESSAGE – Fun is inclusive and abundant.

What **ACTION** do you need to take? Capture it here...

8. Fun is a great surprise

You might think you may be able to give a small bonus this quarter after all. Don't reveal it, there are another two months to go anyway. Announce it when the time is right – the impact will be huge.

KEY MESSAGE – Fun is even more powerful when it is a great old-fashioned surprise.

What **ACTION** do you need to take? Capture it here...

9. Fun is an excuse such as birthdays

Find out birthdays, buy the team a cake with candles, get a crowd, sing happy birthday. Then get back to work.

KEY MESSAGE – Remember individuals; birthdays are ideal.

What **ACTION** do you need to take? Capture it here...

10. Fun is celebrating success

If the big order has come in have a quick blast of 'We are the Champions' in the sales office. If accounts have got debtor days down from 44 last month to 36 this month get a big box of chocolates for the team.

KEY MESSAGE – Reward the behaviours you are seeking.

What **ACTION** do you need to take? Capture it here...

11. Fun keeps your team healthy

Stress stops people being at their best, seems to accelerate illness and consequently increases sick days. Encourage a constant good mood.

KEY MESSAGE – Keep the mood in the office 'good to great'.

What **ACTION** do you need to take? Capture it here...

12. Fun is a state of mind

However bad it gets, there will always be a way out. Keep your sanity and above all keep your sense of humour. Be especially vigilant if you do a lot of work on your own, or run a tiny business solely dependent on you. A network of like-minded individuals facing similar challenges that you can talk to is vital.

KEY MESSAGE – Keep your perspective: it's only work.

What **ACTION** do you need to take? Capture it here...

Your people are only human. They'll work hard and you will work hard, but without some fun what's it all for? Make sure fun is part of the job.

12. Creativity

● ●

The consensus is that the tough times have arrived, that it will hit all sectors and that it is going to get worse before it gets better. We need to get really creative.

UNLEASH YOUR CREATIVE SIDE

Necessity is the mother of invention. Think about bundles, deals and new ways of doing things. You'll be surprised at how tough times times can create some long-needed breakthroughs. Here's how.

1. Yes, you are creative

You are going to need to be very creative during these tough times. You will need to think of new ways to make and save money. Find good reasons for suppliers and clients to continue to work with you. Be imaginative with your funding. Break some long-lasting patterns that are holding you back. What's really holding you back is that you think you are not creative. So let's be clear: anyone can be creative, but like any skill it needs a bit of practice, a bit of time to get to full power. Let's consider how we can accelerate that process.

KEY MESSAGE – You need to be creative and you *are* creative.

What **ACTION** do you need to take? Capture it here...

2. Accelerate creativity by asking questions

The more provocative your questions, the better. What if we got rid of the sales force and sold simply via the net? What if we got rid of the office and everybody worked from home in a virtual team? What if we got out of the garden centre business and turned the site into an organic farm? What if we created an authentic Milanese cafe right in the centre of town? What if our restaurant only had one set meal each night, but it was different each night? What if the gym membership included the use of a fitness coach, which ensured success and reduced the number of leavers. What if...?

KEY MESSAGE – Ask provocative questions to break the status quo.

What **ACTION** do you need to take? Capture it here...

3. Accelerate creativity by brainstorming

You need flipcharts, marker pens, post-it notes and masking tape. Encapsulate the issue on which you wish to generate ideas and give people time to think of as many ideas as possible. What helps?

- A little warm-up first such as, 'Fifteen uses for an old paper coffee cup, please'.

- A target such as, 'We need fifty ideas collectively'.

- Being clear about the subject. Not necessarily 'How can we reduce costs', perhaps but 'How can we save money?'

- Being non-judgemental. The silly, strange and off-the-wall ideas often lead the brain to the breakthrough idea.

KEY MESSAGE – Brainstorm, but do it properly.

What **ACTION** do you need to take? Capture it here...

4. Accelerate creativity by using an established technique

Remember Edward de Bono's 'Six Thinking Hats' technique? Putting on a given 'hat' allows you to get into another mode without fear of criticism. The hats are:

- White for seeking facts and knowledge, e.g. 'How much are we currently losing per day because of late payers?'

- Black for negative and pessimistic but logical thinking, e.g. 'Sending a solicitor's letter won't make a blind bit of difference – it hasn't in the past'.

- Yellow for upbeat and optimistic but logical thought, e.g. 'I think we need to get Mary who is absolutely charming to ring them up and be polite and persistent'.

- Red for speaking from the heart, when there's no need to be logical e.g. 'Stuff them all – hand them over to a debt collector once they're past sixty days, we don't want them anyway'.

- Green for fresh, outside-the-box thinking, e.g. 'Let's start asking all new clients for an upfront part payment; the interest we earn on that will pay for dedicated chasing of late accounts'.

- Blue for overview and process; working out how you will run this thing, e.g. 'Let's brainstorm for twenty minutes, then agree a plan of action for ten minutes'.

KEY MESSAGE – Consider getting out the six hats when you have a problem.

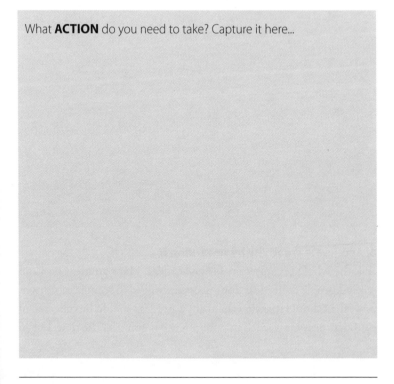

What **ACTION** do you need to take? Capture it here...

5. Accelerate creativity by data deprivation

Phone, text, email, vmail, fax, correspondence, reports, news, TV and radio, conversation, debate, discussion, argument, traffic, hassle – the potential for overload is huge. Never mind the potential physiological damage, it's not good for your creativity. Take a period of time and do absolutely nothing. No conversation, no texting. Perhaps just walk and think. The ideas will come flooding to you. Do it regularly.

KEY MESSAGE – Build at least ten minutes of sheer nothing into every day to boost your creativity.

What **ACTION** do you need to take? Capture it here...

6. Accelerate creativity by rewarding it

Ask the whole organisation for great ideas. Have an ideas box and remind people their ideas don't necessarily need to seem feasible right now; they should mention them anyway. Ideas should be collected in confidence and rewarded in public. Keep it going all the time, but to focus people's minds have a topic of the week, for example, 'How can we reduce shipping costs?'

KEY MESSAGE – Reward great ideas.

What **ACTION** do you need to take? Capture it here...

7. Accelerate creativity by change

Reorganise the office. Move marketing into the sales office; move administrative support into the reception area. Change is unsettling but this can boost fresh thinking and energy.

KEY MESSAGE – Shake up their thinking by shaking up their world.

What **ACTION** do you need to take? Capture it here...

8. Accelerate creativity by getting out of the office

Don't pay for this privilege of course. Find our when your local coffee bar is quiet and take your team out for a coffee. Brief them while walking there, brainstorm while having your drink and agree actions on the walk back.

KEY MESSAGE – A change of scene can boost creativity.

What **ACTION** do you need to take? Capture it here...

9. Accelerate creativity by asking

Ask your colleagues, your network, your customer, your supplier, your mum, the lecturer who led your critical thinking module on the MBA, the bank manager. Email the journalist who wrote the excellent article in last week's paper. They may or may not be able to help. But you won't know unless you ask.

KEY MESSAGE – Ask questions to boost your ideas bank.

What **ACTION** do you need to take? Capture it here...

10. Accelerate creativity by doing something with the ideas

Whatever the format of the session capture and record the ideas carefully. Weigh them up and if you agree they are worth pursuing, build them into an action plan.

> **KEY MESSAGE – Do something** as a result of your creativity.

What **ACTION** do you need to take? Capture it here...

11. Innovation = creativity + action

If there is one thing most strategy experts agree on, it's that you must innovate to survive this slow down. Innovation is about fresh thinking coupled with clear action. They require different modes of thinking which is why companies often gravitate to one or other side of the equation. Develop your team of people so that you can both create and act.

KEY MESSAGE – Make sure you can fulfil both parts of the innovation equation.

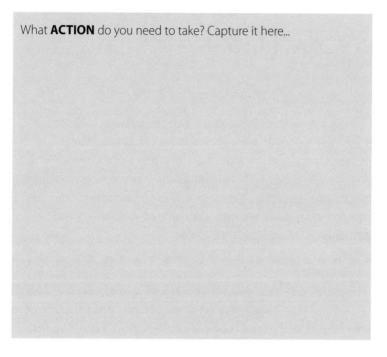

What **ACTION** do you need to take? Capture it here...

Never will you need to be more imaginative and creative than now, whether it's marketing campaigns, sales deals, resourcing or any other aspect of your business. But of course you're up for that, aren't you?

13. Processes and systems

'The BBC's economics editor said that the poor figures from the High Street were a signal that the UK would not completely escape economic problems. "I'm afraid that this will be a difficult year even if it goes well," he explained. "There's little point in hoping that government or consumer spending can change that. Even if we put ourselves in the lap of the gods, we won't avoid some kind of slowdown in 2008".'
BBC News on bbc.co.uk, 18 January 2008

● ●

The consensus is that the tough times have arrived, that it will hit all sectors and that it is going to get worse before it gets better. To be at your best, all of the time, you need excellent processes and systems in place.

BRING ON THE GEEKS
Assemble a team to look into the fine details of company systems and processes. Which systems are leaky and let you and the customers down? What is twenty-two cobbled-together processes and should be just three? You must get your processes to work with you not against you. Here's how.

1. Processes and systems?
Standardised methods of doing things, which save everybody time and ensure key monitoring and running of the business, should happen

automatically and make it easier to be successful. Examples might include a regular weekly meeting to review the prospect pipeline, or expenses guidelines. It takes a bit of time to set these up, but once done they look after themselves and pay for themselves many times over: that's a good process or system. They are particularly invaluable during tough times when resources are tight and everything counts.

KEY MESSAGE – Define your essential processes and systems now. Ensure your current ones are working.

What **ACTION** do you need to take? Capture it here...

2. Sales System 1

Create a process which allows you to manage the flow of business from prospect status through to won business. This is most easily done through some kind of simply designed form, which may eventually, once it is tried and tested, become an online tool. The essential part of the process is the prospect review, at which each sales person is asked to be accountable for her order prospects before a panel. Is the prospect qualified, when will they come in, what margin will they generate? It's a demanding session for all concerned but the best salespeople learn to appreciate the process, and it certainly weeds out those who are not performing. Most importantly, through discussion and quizzing, you should get a very good idea of the amount and quality of business in the pipeline. You will have an idea of what might actually materialise rather than relying on the naive optimism of any individual.

KEY MESSAGE – Start prospect reviews immediately.

What **ACTION** do you need to take? Capture it here...

3. Sales System 2

Make it easy to generate quotes. Create templates for rapid assembly of the best proposals. Ensure you standardise terms and conditions and legal statements according to the advice of your experts. Ensure they look good, both on paper if they arrive in the post and on screen if they arrive as an attachment.

KEY MESSAGE – Standardise the quote and proposal.

What **ACTION** do you need to take? Capture it here...

4. Sales System 3

Have a clear price list and ensure it is fully understood. Ensure that discounting policies are documented and applied. Answer the following questions:

▪ Who has authority for discounting?

▪ How is the level of discounting monitored?

▪ What incentives are there for preserving margin?

KEY MESSAGE – Regularly update the price list and ensure that discounting policies are understood.

What **ACTION** do you need to take? Capture it here...

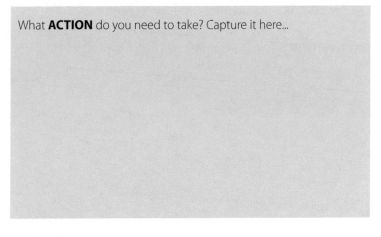

5. Sales System 4

Ensure there is a clear system for tracking every prospect and that they are appropriately followed up, depending on the value of business. In financially tricky times, every piece of business counts. Nobody can afford to lose business because they forgot to follow up on the promised day or the sales person was ill.

KEY MESSAGE – Follow up all business.

What **ACTION** do you need to take? Capture it here...

6. Sales System 5

Celebrate success. Announce wins, good deals and achieved revenue targets. Always remember that the biggest motivator of people is the feeling that they are appreciated.

KEY MESSAGE – Make a fuss of success.

What **ACTION** do you need to take? Capture it here...

7. Marketing System 1

The planning round. Competitive edge is derived from the powerful combination of strategy and implementation of marketing, communication, pricing and product development plans. Set dates in the diary well in advance so a 'planning round' can run smoothly and continuously with all concerned aware of dates and responsibilities.

KEY MESSAGE – 'Diarise' the planning round.

What **ACTION** do you need to take? Capture it here...

8. Marketing System 2

Create simple documentation which captures the main components of the marketing strategy (e.g. Kotler's 4Ps and appropriate SWOT analyses). Support these with implementation plans showing actions, milestones and responsibilities.

KEY MESSAGE – Create a marketing bible.

What **ACTION** do you need to take? Capture it here...

9. Ideas, suggestions, complaints and review system

Create a simple system for encouraging all members of the organisation to contribute great ideas and feedback. Clearly one route for these is via their line-manager and that should be used where the suggested improvement is specific and local (e.g. Why don't we ask just one person to be responsible for that document from when it comes into the office until it has been fulfilled). For wider-ranging ideas (e.g. Why don't we implement flexitime for anyone willing to work an extra thirty minutes at no extra pay for the next six months?) or complaints (e.g., This organisation still has too much hierarchy, no wonder we never get anything done) the possibility of anonymity has advantages. Clearly great ideas should be rewarded. Contributions should be reviewed weekly.

KEY MESSAGE – Make it easy to suggest. Make it easy to improve. Make it easy to complain.

What **ACTION** do you need to take? Capture it here...

10. Invoicing systems

Clearly invoices are the lifeblood of the organisation. There must be a process which is followed for:

- Prompt issue of invoices (with clear layout, explanation of payment terms and contact details for queries);

- Checking invoices to ensure no errors;

- Prompt posting of invoices;

- Checking receipt of invoices (very important in recessionary times where organisations will do anything they can to delay payment);

- Chasing invoices if payment is not received on the correct date and

- Applying appropriate polite pressure until payment is received.

KEY MESSAGE – Chase the money you are owed!

What **ACTION** do you need to take? Capture it here...

11. The staff handbook

Dull or corporate it may be but it's indispensable for containing costs and resolving simple disputes over policy. All kinds of things can go in here from induction procedure to resignation details. What you should be most concerned with when it comes to managing your business in tough times is getting a good expenses guidelines policy (use of credit cards, which hotels are acceptable, what standard of travel can be used) and a clear company confidentiality policy (e.g. if a client asks how well you are doing and you have just had your most atrocious quarter yet, what's the company line?).

KEY MESSAGE – Creating your handbook is a priority.

What **ACTION** do you need to take? Capture it here...

12. Security systems

Don't assume anything. We often forget how much information is contained in our databases. How are your prospect and account information protected?

KEY MESSAGE – Ensure top security, especially for the 'soft' stuff.

What **ACTION** do you need to take? Capture it here...

13. Beat the system

Whatever system you create to protect your business, you know that someone will find a way to beat it. This won't necessarily be in a malevolent way, they just want to get their job done and if they can avoid some paperwork then they'll be happier. Don't allow it, otherwise you'll start to wonder where your money is leaking away. Start with education; explain that the new policy (e.g. on expenses) has not become draconian, it's simply that there is an opportunity to save a lot of money with little hardship for anyone. Here are three common examples where the system is easily broken:

- Finance: credit cards are used for purchasing items which should have purchase order numbers and appropriate authorisation.

- Security: valuable databases are taken offsite on laptops.

- Resources: temporary staff are bought by the day although there is a strict no headcount increase policy.

KEY MESSAGE – How would you beat the system? Now stop it!

What **ACTION** do you need to take? Capture it here...

14. Systems thinking

If there is one time you need kaizen (continuous improvement thinking) it is now. Keep asking: how can we make this better, faster and easier for both us and the customer?

KEY MESSAGE – Kaizen.

What **ACTION** do you need to take? Capture it here...

Everything needs a process: once processes are in place you can concentrate on what you are good at, which is leading. It's leadership which will pull the organisation through: vision, inspiration and tough decision-making. Set up great processes so that you can lead.

14. Management

'More than three in four Americans believe the U.S. economy is already in a recession, or will be sometime in 2008 … Only 19 percent of 1000 Americans surveyed believe the nation will avoid a recession, while 57 percent believe that there will be a downturn this year. Another 19 percent believe the nation is already in a recession. What's worse for the economic outlook, just about half of those surveyed say that they've cut back their spending compared to last year. These results indicate a far gloomier outlook than economists anticipated.'
Chris Isidore, **CNNMoney.com**, 22 January 2008

● ●

The consensus is that the tough times have arrived, that it will hit all sectors and that it is going to get worse before it gets better. You need a team effort to get through this and that will depend very much upon how you, the management, are viewed.

HOW ARE YOU MANAGING?

You're going to have to be prepared to get your hands dirty. If you cancel the free coffee machine for the team, what's your hardship? You must be part of the tough time you are asking others to endure. Here's how.

1. A lot of it is psychology

This doesn't mean it's not important. When times are tough, we all need to make sacrifices. The emphasis your people want to hear is on *all*. You'll be asking a lot of people to make sacrifices, especially if you run a larger organisation. No bonuses, perhaps. Salary increases on hold, possibly. Some redundancies, maybe. Certainly a definite loss of security. What about you? Are you making sacrifices? Of course you are. The buck stops with you. You may still drive a BMW, but it's meaningless if the whole business collapses. But not everyone will see it that way: they still see the smart cars and the ability to manage one's own time. You must communicate the contributions that everybody is being asked to make and is making. You do want to avoid the perception that 'it's all right for them in their fancy suits and office, we'll be the first to go when times get really tough'. And how do you do that? Read on.

KEY MESSAGE – Perception is reality.

What **ACTION** do you need to take? Capture it here...

2. Pack boxes, but...

Create an accurate perception of what's going on by being around, by getting close, by avoiding being or being seen to be remote. Talk to the 'troops', get onto the shop floor, spend some time in the call centre, go out on a call with a rep, get close, talk and show that you are human. Of course you could pack those boxes but that isn't (or certainly shouldn't be) a good use of your time. It is worth finding out if they have all they need to pack boxes, if they have any particular challenges or even if they have any ideas for making the processes simpler or faster.

KEY MESSAGE – Be around.

What **ACTION** do you need to take? Capture it here...

3. Remove barriers between people

Maybe this is a great time to break down some of those unnecessary barriers caused by issues such as the rows of (often unused) reserved car-parking spaces, the separate canteens and the different grading systems. What if a few key changes in that area of the business were announced at the monthly meeting to show you are for real? Such changes should also be great in aiding communication, improving idea transfer and boosting morale.

KEY MESSAGE – Break down those unnecessary barriers.

What **ACTION** do you need to take? Capture it here...

4. Leadership

Your people need leading. Leadership is about providing them with a vision beyond this painful year. All good leadership is about hope. That hope will come from a great strategy which sounds real and practical for this year and beyond. Great leadership is about energising people. They enjoy you being around and they enjoy your talks at the monthly meeting. Great leaders communicate, so tell it as it is.

KEY MESSAGE – Lead, now more than ever.

What **ACTION** do you need to take? Capture it here...

5. Management

Management is concerned with day-to-day implementation of the plan. It is about getting things done and making stuff happen. Make sure your managers and team leaders are:

■ Having regular team meetings to motivate, tackle issues and blockers and keep their people on track;

■ Coaching their people one-to-one to develop the best skills possible;

■ Ensuring their people are absolutely focused on what needs to be done to turn the business around;

■ Catching people doings things right;

■ Running mini-training sessions;

■ Keeping close to all the necessary processes to identify how things might be improved.

KEY MESSAGE – Manage, now more than ever.

What **ACTION** do you need to take? Capture it here...

6. Empower

Give your people SMART (**s**pecific, **m**easurable, **a**chievable, **r**ealistic and **t**ime-bound) objectives. Train them, coach them and motivate them. Then, and this is the hard part, let go. Why don't you want to do that? Three suggestions:

1. They make mistakes. No, they *learn*. If they make a mistake, treat it as a learning experience and make sure it doesn't happen again. If reviewed properly, it won't.

2. They may become as good as or better than you. Excellent, that's known as succession planning, and how can you be promoted post-recession if you don't have someone to do your job?

3. Ego. We like to feel in control. But if you let go you will become even more effective.

KEY MESSAGE – Empower, now more than ever.

What **ACTION** do you need to take? Capture it here...

7. Grow your people

There are a lot of carrots you will not be able to dangle this year: salary increases, bonuses, staff parties, generous expenses. Perhaps there will be fewer training courses. But you can provide one thing which motivates everyone: growth and challenge. It needs to be appropriate for the individual: one person's growth opportunity is starting her own business, another's is turning around the accounts department, another's is getting 100% accurate order fulfilment statistics after months of running at around 87%. But give the responsibility to them. You are low on resources. Fewer people need to do more work. Managers are expensive so empower. Ask people to be better at self-managing and they will be. And they will enjoy it.

KEY MESSAGE – Grow your people through challenge, not comfort.

What **ACTION** do you need to take? Capture it here...

· ·

Get hands-on: you will learn, you will motivate and you will inspire.
That's it!

15. Invest

'The bears are loose. In financial market speak, bears are economic pessimists. And this morning, nearly every speaker was deeply concerned about the state of the global economy. We won't see a global recession, everybody agreed, but if the panellists were right, then the United States and – to a lesser extent – Europe are in for a really rough ride.'
Tim Weber reporting from the World Economic forum, **BBC news on bbc.co.uk**, 23 January 2008

● ●

The consensus is that the tough times have arrived, that it will hit all sectors and that it is going to get worse before it gets better. To be at your best, all of the time, you need to do exactly the opposite of what most people will be doing: you need to invest.

BE CONTRARY

It's really tempting to take away, to strip down, but believe me you need invest. Keep the marketing and training budgets. Just spend them a lot more wisely. You must invest for the future. Here's how.

1. Invest

It is very tempting to not invest in tough times, to cancel the technology upgrade, as well as all the newspapers, to run the stationery cupboard to empty, to manage only buying clients and forget the others, to overwork. But it just doesn't work. Markets will catch up with you and you will be under-prepared to respond to recovery, you will have a demotivated workforce and you will be missing opportunities. Of course you need to stop waste and buy more carefully. You could also try some just in time delivery practice and cut off non-essential training as long as you also make the necessary investments. Your business will die otherwise.

KEY MESSAGE – Invest or die.

What **ACTION** do you need to take? Capture it here...

2. Invest in people 1: well-being
Ensure people feel at their best doing their jobs. Boost their well-being. They don't need pampering, but they may need air conditioning. They don't need spoiling but maybe they do need a serviceable office chair. Sort out the basics, also known as hygiene factors.

KEY MESSAGE – Sort the basics of well-being in your workplace.

What **ACTION** do you need to take? Capture it here...

3. Invest in people 2: development

The training budget may well be slashed, but that doesn't stop development. Create a learning library and stock it with books purchased with some of your saved training budget. Ask people to share useful ideas from their reading at the team meeting. Get a few audiobooks for people to listen to in the car on the way to meetings. Remind your team leaders how to coach, and do some coaching yourself. Trained people work better. Better work equals more profit.

KEY MESSAGE – Train and coach.

What **ACTION** do you need to take? Capture it here...

4. Invest in people 3: motivation

Ensure reviews continue, even if pay discussions are on hold. There is still plenty to talk about: How are they getting on? Where do they want to take their careers? What challenges do they have in their job? What would they like from the company? What would the company like from them? Detail actions, write it up and implement the results.

KEY MESSAGE – Find out what makes them tick.

What **ACTION** do you need to take? Capture it here...

5. Invest in key equipment

Don't wait until it falls apart. Why lose the business simply because you can't create a quality proposal as your colour printer is down and nobody renewed the maintenance contract. You know the sort of thing.

> **KEY MESSAGE – Identify equipment** essential to your business and maintain and update it.

What **ACTION** do you need to take? Capture it here...

6. Invest in technology, especially systems

Technology is getting cheaper and cleverer and it means you can make do with fewer people. Give it loads of attention, buy carefully and consider how investment in technology could help you through this recession. You should be offered some good deals too, as nobody else is buying.

KEY MESSAGE – Invest to save.

What **ACTION** do you need to take? Capture it here...

7. Invest in your channels

Never assume that you are going to get business even from people you feel have no choice but to buy from you. Thank them for their business and give them appropriate attention. Be aware of taking your eye off the ball and spending too much time as 'hunter' and not enough time as 'farmer'. Keep considering other channels. If you have traditionally been direct, could it work to try the indirect route? If you normally sell only through the internet, could it work to have a store somewhere?

KEY MESSAGE – How else could you access business?

What **ACTION** do you need to take? Capture it here...

8. Invest in your suppliers

There are a few of your current suppliers that you would be in a mess without. Stay close, meet with them and return their calls. If there are going to be payment problems, keep them informed.

KEY MESSAGE – Keep talking.

What **ACTION** do you need to take? Capture it here...

9. Invest in your clients

Raise your standards. You are confident that they think you are good. But what would it take for them to think you are brilliant? What would it take to make the product so good that price sensitivity would drop away? That's the kind of thinking and investment in the client that needs to be done.

KEY MESSAGE – Knock their socks off.

What **ACTION** do you need to take? Capture it here...

10. Invest in your image

The web site needs an update, the e-newsletter is dreary and the local paper never talks about you because you 'fell out' with the editor. Time to change. Find some cheap but good web designer to create a simple but elegant site. Scrap the newsletter. Ring up the paper and grovel if you have to.

KEY MESSAGE – Think image.

What **ACTION** do you need to take? Capture it here...

11. Invest in you

Stay healthy: get quality sleep, it tends to go first in troubled times. Stay fit: walking is easy and keeps you creative, too. Keep thinking: strive for continuous improvement. Keep leading: inspire your people to give their best. Be creative: keep asking those 'what if?' questions. Be an innovator and make this organisation more resilient.

KEY MESSAGE – You are an investment too.

What **ACTION** do you need to take? Capture it here...

Your competitors aren't doing it, they are panicking. But through selective and careful investing, your standards are only going to get higher. You are becoming more and more attractive to deal with. And just wait until this slump is over!

16. Talk is cheap

'Most economists…are looking for a relatively short and mild downturn, perhaps lasting only two or three quarters. But many of those same economists say they also can envision a worst-case scenario where spending by consumers and businesses falls off sharply, unemployment heads higher than normal during a typical recession and housing and credit market problems worsen.'
Chris Isidore, ***CNN money.com***, 24 January 2008

● ●

The consensus is that the tough times have arrived, that it will hit all sectors and that it is going to get worse before it gets better. Better knuckle under then – and that means less chat, more action.

JUST DO IT!
Action is needed. Reward positive action, talk down problems, talk up success. You must become Mr Motivator. Here's how.

1. Less chat, more action
Who doesn't love a good chat, a bit of a gossip, even a real moan at times? Or what about a true rant? Yes, they are good fun, probably therapeutic and help let off steam but they don't get the job done. Do anything and everything you can to keep people focused on the task in hand. Just imagine what would happen if you could reclaim that 20% of the day which disappears on gossip.

KEY MESSAGE – Remind everyone that chat is good but at the right time and in the right place.

What **ACTION** do you need to take? Capture it here...

2. Make a rule

To achieve less chat and more action, ask people to follow this rule: do not talk negatively about someone when that person is not present. Explain why it is important, that without absolute trust a team cannot be effective and that the quickest way to break trust is to talk about a person behind their back. You will find everyone buys into this idea (that doesn't mean they find it easy to implement) and is keen to practise it. Once people follow this rule, they find that much of the gossiping, complaining and ranting goes away. The new forum for such problems becomes the team meeting where the problem can be solved more quickly.

KEY MESSAGE – Get everybody to follow one simple rule.

What **ACTION** do you need to take? Capture it here...

3. Office layout

Open plan is the bugbear of anyone trying to get on with some work but as a layout it is cheap. Go to your second-hand office furniture merchants (there will be plenty during a recession), buy up some sizeable screens and place them strategically around the office. Don't stop light flow, don't 'pen' people in cubicles, just create a few sound barriers. People will love you for it. They will now chat in the kitchen or outside the office rather than while someone is on the phone trying to chase overdue accounts (hard enough to do under the best circumstances).

KEY MESSAGE – Break up the open plan.

What **ACTION** do you need to take? Capture it here...

4. Give a big picture, a purpose

Make sure every team knows its big goal for the month: close 60 orders, reduce debtor days from 37 to 31, release the product upgrade to New Zealand, find one new client each week during April. Update it every month.

KEY MESSAGE – Define the team purpose.

What **ACTION** do you need to take? Capture it here...

5. Give clear, small and manageable goals to each person

Break those big monthly goals into individual weekly and daily tasks. For example, 'Sally, you need to ring those customers and discover the status of each invoice'; 'Tim, you need to ring around serviced offices and find out their best deal for three offices for twenty people'.

KEY MESSAGE – Provide clear daily and weekly task lists for everyone.

What **ACTION** do you need to take? Capture it here...

6. It's a decision not a job title

Ask people to do their bit. It may not be in their job title, it may not be what they were employed to do and they probably won't be getting paid extra for it. But it does mean they have a job. Don't be overly melodramatic, but remind them that nothing can be assumed.

KEY MESSAGE – Your value to the company is based on actions not job title.

What **ACTION** do you need to take? Capture it here...

7. Daily action meetings

Meet your management team every morning before the phones start ringing. Make it short and to the point. Start with your report, then listen to all of your managers' reports. Use the headings good news (what's gone well), challenges (any difficulties) and actions (how those difficulties are being resolved). Ask them to go off and do the same with their teams, until the whole company is working on a clear task-driven daily basis.

KEY MESSAGE – Roll-out your daily briefing.

What **ACTION** do you need to take? Capture it here...

8. Project plans

Insist that big goals are described by formal project plans. If you want to reduce staff costs by 35%, release your latest product 3 months early or increase market share by 7% among the 16–25 age range you need to project manage. If that skill isn't owned by your company, get someone trained. The course fee will be repaid many times over in successful execution.

KEY MESSAGE – Get project management trained.

What **ACTION** do you need to take? Capture it here...

9. Raise standards

There's poor, there's OK and there's excellent. You won't be poor for long because you will be out of business. You could struggle along at OK for a while but it will be really painful. Don't do it. Talk excellence, act excellence, be excellent. As part of the review and coaching process, get managers to describe what each of those levels would look like for each job and insist on excellent. Why? It'll be fun, and your company will become remarkable (in the true sense of the word, 'worth remarking upon').

KEY MESSAGE – Raise standards and become remarkable.

What **ACTION** do you need to take? Capture it here...

10. Don't be too nice

Don't be too nasty either. To change a few behaviours and raise a few standards you're going to have to be pretty firm a lot of the time. You'll need to be assertive. Do it. You can't afford to be too nice to the people who are letting you down. On the other hand, stay balanced. For some, whatever you say or do, it's still 'just a job' but as long as they do it really well, that's fine.

KEY MESSAGE – Be firm and assertive but not too nasty.

What **ACTION** do you need to take? Capture it here...

11. Celebrate success

Success breeds success. When you are successful, celebrate. Celebrate the win, congratulate the team and congratulate the individual. And go off and do it again.

KEY MESSAGE – Catch the most positive of business behaviours: success.

What **ACTION** do you need to take? Capture it here...

Do everything you can to reduce unnecessary chat and increase purposeful action. Purposeful action leads to great results and great results mean surviving this downturn. That's what everybody in your organisation wants, they just need reminding!

17. Relax

Relax, it really will be OK and you will come out of it leaner, meaner and stronger.

HOW CAN YOU BE SURE?

It really is going to be OK because you are a smart person and having read this book you are clearly serious about taking action. I don't know what stage the slump will be in when you read this. It may still be slipping deeper; it may have stabilised, there may even be evidence that we are coming out of it. It doesn't matter. What is important is how it is affecting your business. Someone else's end of tough times could be the start of yours. The thing to do now is to get a plan and this blueprint will enable you to do that.

31 reasons why you can relax

1. Checklist 1 reminded you what you need to do about money. You're going to be ahead of the game because you know how much you have and how much you are making. And you'll know what those processes are costing you. You'll have control systems in place. Everyone will be a lot more careful about the dangerous game of discounting.

2. You are staying fit! Your energy, resilience and ability to cope with the mental pressure and fatigue of this downturn is essential. You have decided to look after yourself with the basic practices of proper sleep, taking time out, eating sensibly and taking some simple cardiovascular exercise.

3. Checklist 2 reminded you that this is not a time for 'possibly' or 'maybe' or 'let me think about it'. This is a time to make and be

seen to be making tough decisions. OK, you may make a few mistakes but at least in making those decisions you are getting feedback, and with that feedback you can adjust your company's direction.

4. You have invested in a whiteboard. Something which you stare at every day which lists the key action points you and your team have extracted from this book.

5. Checklist 3 reminded you to get a handle on the facts, which you have done. You are also being creative and using your imagination, but basing it on the facts. With facts you are able to argue your case to the bank manager, decide which product lines to discontinue and see who's performing in the sales team.

6. You are breaking patterns and assumptions all the time.

7. Checklist 4 prompted you to ensure that people are feeling motivated, cared for and focused.

8. You act success. You are resourceful, not arrogant. You are upbeat, not naively positive. People like to deal with you. They'll work well for you.

9. Checklist 5 helped you to get your selling systems in place. You've reduced discounting and are negotiating properly. You've been bold and introduced some premium prices. Cool.

10. You think. A lot more.

11. Checklist 6 made you think about real marketing, proper pricing strategy, product positioning and clear communications. Fantastic.

12. You're going to make more use of local colleges when looking for smart, cheap resources and thinking.

13. Checklist 7 helped you to sort out the basics, from telephone answering to invoicing, to car parking spots.

14. The company now runs to a plan. And that plan has actions. And those actions are owned by individuals.

15. Checklist 8 reminded you to talk to people: your staff, your suppliers and your clients. It's amazing how much you are achieving now that you communicate clearly and regularly and hence build trust.

16. You are networking again.

17. Checklist 9 reminded you that at the very least what is bad for someone else may be good for you. You are alert to some amazing opportunities.

18. You've always got a business book on the go and since your key market information RSS feeds to your computer directly you're going to be on top of these markets.

19. Checklist 10 taught you the subtle difference between 'in' and 'on' time. More importantly, you are now using it.

20. You are seen about your business. You are now seen doing stuff, helping, congratulating and leading by example. Plus you really know what is going on.

21. Checklist 11 has prompted you to remember that fun is (to a certain degree) what it is all about. You're having fun again. Excellent.

22. You regularly take a walk to put things in perspective. If it's around the business park, so be it. If it can be across the park, even better. But when you're a walker nothing seems quite so bad.

23. The actions you took away from checklist 12 mean that your organisation has never been more creative than it's being now. That's because in the past you hadn't clicked that creativity was the basis of innovation and innovation is the only way to survive in a global economy, particularly one that's gone phut.

24. Some days (though only to yourself) you'll admit that although tough times are hard work, and at times downright scary, it's what you needed. You've never been more clear about what you are about as a company, never been better at selling and marketing. And at last you feel you have some robust business plans.

25. Checklist 13 has got you in control of current systems and helped you introduce missing systems so that what doesn't require brain power or manual work can now be automated.

26. A paper and pencil are keeping you focused. Every day, you take a postcard and rule it (landscape) down the middle. The left hand side is 'in' (important + urgent) time, the right hand side is 'on' (important + investing) time. You distribute your vital few task lists across the two sides. You ensure that at the start of this process it's strongly 'in', but as things progress you are moving to work 'on' your business.

27. Checklist 14 has ensured you are hands-on and have dropped any special treatment for management. And to be honest, you feel a whole lot better for it. There's no 'us and them', there's a great team spirit and you know there's no money being wasted on ego and vanity.

28. Each day you ask what are the vital few, the Pareto tasks for today (named after the inventor of the 80/20 principle). In other words, you ask which 20% of your efforts tends to generate 80% of the results, and then you do these tasks. You make sure every

one of your people is following that practice and not being distracted by the many trivial tasks.

29. Checklist 15 has got you investing. You are not going to be one of those people who strips the whole organisation to nothing and runs on vapour and then wonders why you are stuck in the wilderness without a map. You are investing to keep going and investing in preparation for take-off when markets bounce back.

30. You have booked a break. You are working very hard, you have achieved a huge amount so you deserve a break. Enjoy it and ensure things remain in healthy perspective.

31. Checklist 16 has got you acting rather than just talking. It's reminded you that a decision is not a decision until you take an action. It's got you loving task lists and execution plans. That's not only cool, it's also a very good reason why you can relax.

So now you see why you can relax – you are ahead of the game. You are at an extreme of the bell curve. You know what you are trying to do. You are in control. You have plans and you can and are getting the support of those you need. Get back to work. Get back to life. Relax. It'll all be OK.

Index